A NIACE POLICY DISCUSSION PAPER

Demography and Older Learners

Approaches to a new policy challenge

Edited by Alan Tuckett and Alec McAulay
with contributions from Stephen McNair, Tom Schuller, Jim Soulsby and Judith Summers

promoting adult learning

promoting adult learning

©2005 National Institute of Adult Continuing Education
(England and Wales)

21 De Montfort Street
Leicester
LE1 7GE

Company registration no. 2603322
Charity registration no. 1002775

NIACE has a broad remit to promote lifelong learning opportunities for
adults. NIACE works to develop increased participation in education and
training, particularly for those who do not have easy access because of class,
gender, age, race, language and culture, learning difficulties or disabilities, or
insufficient financial resources.

You can find NIACE online at **www.niace.org.uk**

Cataloguing in Publication Data
A CIP record of this title is available from the British Library

Designed and typeset by Patrick Armstrong, Book Production Services,
London
Print and bound in the UK by Latimer Trend

ISBN: 1 86201 240 7

Contents

Contents

Introduction

Alan Tuckett, Director of NIACE

Demography, globalisation and technological change make for a heady mix that impacts on all our lives. To date that is most apparent in pensions policy. Mid-life and older workers suddenly find their expectations of security in older age turn soft as final salary pensions schemes close, and risk transfers from employer to individual. Meanwhile, young people are exhorted to start saving now to have enough in a pension pot to avoid poverty in later life. This comes on top of rising student loan debt, and the potential for a rising tax burden to meet the care needs of today's elders.

In this debate education has been largely missing – yet the same impact can be expected, particularly for older people. This NIACE policy discussion paper aims to rectify that omission. As longevity has increased, the dependency ratio (the number of workers sharing the cost of supporting each person outside the workforce) has shrunk dramatically. That means each of us in work has to be more productive, putting another premium on skills to add to the pressures that come from increasing global competition.

There is also the prospect of a major labour shortage over the next decade, as the post-war generation of workers who make and mend things come up for retirement.

As figure 1 shows, the projected net increase of 2.1 million jobs between 1999 and 2010 requires 13.5 million new workers, owing to the departure of more than 11 million of the 1999 workforce through retirement, sickness, death or other reasons. Only one-third or so of the new workers will come from indigenous new young entrants to the national workforce: the balance will have to be drawn from a combination of three sources: a further increase in the proportion of women in the workforce (and Britain already has a high proportion by international standards); net in-migration (British public opinion stubbornly opposes in-migrants' taking of skilled and unskilled jobs, and equity demands that in-migration from less prosperous economies ought not be used to remedy UK skill shortages); and older people staying on in the labour force, or returning to it, or taking up new opportunities.

For many older people this will be an act of choice, but for more a necessity, if they are to avoid an impoverished later life. Yet for many older people learning new skills has not been part of working life.

Increased provision of learning for older people is a perfect example of enlightened self-interest. Societal benefits – home care of elderly and children;

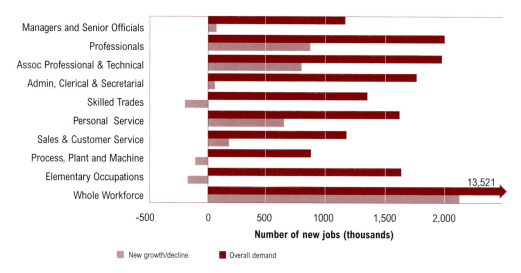

Number of new jobs (thousands)

New growth/decline   Overall demand

Figure 1: Occupational demand to 2010 (Source: Projections of Occupations and Qualifications, IER, 2001)

health benefits; the economic and fiscal interests of the state; and individual financial and personal satisfaction are all served by extending and improving the quality and length of working and active life.

Adult learning is the single most effective means of this extension and improvement. Yet in the substantial literature on policy options for an ageing society it is surprisingly absent.

Changes in the labour market are likely, too, to exacerbate trends in civic life where more and more of the voluntary activity that sustains the fabric of our civic and social lives fall to older people to sustain. Older people are also major contributors to care services – notably to even older people cared for at home. With the labour market sucking in more and more people from the traditional labour market sectors, older people are likely to bear even more of the responsibility for care in the community. This task will grow, too: so far, medical advances have given us longer lives, but have not increased the proportion of the Third Age where we live active lives in good health.

Here learning can play an important role. Learning is, as the Centre for Wider Benefits in Learning has shown, good for your health and longevity. Yet participation in learning among older people is heavily skewed to those who enjoyed learning earlier in their lives. Indeed, the learning divide is at its clearest among older people.

The latest NIACE participation survey highlights the fall-off in participation in learning in later life (figure 2).

What is clear is that for work, and for national and individual economic benefits, for an enriched cultural and civic life, and for the good of your health, learning

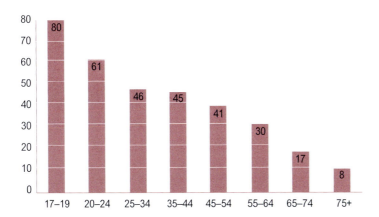

Figure 2: Current/recent participation in adult learning, by age

Base: all respondents=100%

offers benefits in older life. But that case needs to be made powerfully, and in ways that connect with the lives of older people in Britain.

This collection of papers is a contribution to kick-starting policy change – to secure for Britain's elders the education and training policies they have a right to expect, and all of us need to secure.

Tom Schuller's paper 'Demographic challenges: family structures and ageing' sets the context for this collection in a helpful way. It was written some time ago for a different purpose but, having been updated, still provides an excellent overview of the impact of demographic change on a range of our current practices and the extent to which they polarise wealth and poverty. He highlights challenges to current practice, seeking new ways to combine risk, security and responsibility, to release collective funds, to sustain and promote trust and social capital and to secure a different distribution of time and opportunity over the lifecourse. Tom's paper ends with a coda of policy challenges better to meet the needs of older learners.

Whilst Tom's paper looks at the impact of demographic change on everyone, the rest of the contributions look at impact on older learners in particular.

In 'The age of choice: a new agenda for learning and work' Stephen McNair highlights the dramatic differences in freedom of choice and action facing different cohorts of older people in deciding the balance of work and 'not-work' in their lives. He concludes that we need to recognise the diversity of older people, and of firms and sectors; the need to encourage personal autonomy, and the importance of thinking about older people and work to focus on the distinct issues involved in retaining people at work and offering effective opportunities for re-entry.

Judith Summers' paper, 'Fit for purposes: do policies and planning work for older learners?' draws on four local case studies to examine how far provision addresses the need for equity; the need to accommodate changing patterns of working life; the needs of Fourth Age learners, and the ability of the system to respond to the diverse needs of different groups. Her conclusion is that our current provision works only to a limited extent and that a number of modest changes could make a real difference.

If the public policy debate about demography is relatively new, NIACE's commitment to highlighting older learners' needs is not. Jim Soulsby, who has offered an inspirational lead to NIACE's Older & Bolder programme since 1996 reviews that work, and highlights the critical importance of securing joined-up government, if services are to work for older learners. For policy makers, the advice is, in E. M. Forster's memorable phrase, 'Only connect'!

Finally, the papers end with modest proposals to the new Secretary of State for Education and Skills on things she could do quickly to put older learners' needs on the policy agenda.

Like other NIACE Policy Discussion Papers, this one has been reviewed by our Policy Committee, and the papers also informed a joint NIACE/DfES seminar in 2004. It is offered to stimulate argument and debate, and in the belief that older people's learning needs have been marginal too long.

It would be wrong to finish this introduction without recognising the contribution made by Alec McAulay to shaping and steering the whole publication to conclusion. Publishing editors perform a variety of tasks – their contribution can range from a light touch briefing the named author or editor to manager of the production process or, occasionally, to acting as an active shaper of the project. This last has been Alec's function for this publication, and any strengths in the work are his as well as the authors'.

1. Demographic challenges: family structures and ageing

Tom Schuller, CERI OECD Paris

Outline

The key lines of this paper[1] are as follows:

- The patterns of entry into adulthood, of family life and of old age are increasingly variegated, but there is a persistent, quite rigid, sequence of education–work–leisure.

- The UK shares many trends with most or all other industrialised countries. British 'exceptionalism' exists in a number of ways, notably in longer working hours and lower pension commitments.

- Families are changing shape and structure, becoming thinner, longer and looser. They retain most of their established functions, of socialisation, social contact, caring and so on. These need support, especially to maintain trust and communication.

- Polarisation of various kinds – of time, of money and of social contact – is a major issue, over the lifecourse as a whole and across different groups.

- An ageing population should not be equated only with the growth in numbers of older people.

- The ageing of the population does present problems, especially in respect of the emotional, financial and moral strains which result from the growth of the very old, but there is no reason to cast the issue predominantly in negative terms.

- The UK's current low commitment to public pensions offers a huge opportunity for investment in social infrastructure providing positive support across the lifecourse.

- The paper concludes with a menu of challenges:
  > new concepts/vocabulary to suit changing times;
  > integrating assets and benefits to combine risk, security and responsibility;
  > more creative use of collective funds;
  > new forms of personal service delivery;
  > sustaining and promoting trust and social capital;
  > a different distribution of time and opportunity over the lifecourse.

---

1 This paper was originally prepared for a policy debate in 2000. Where necessary and possible, the statistics have been updated, but the substantive issues and arguments, gratifyingly, have not changed.

The population ages; the lifecourse stays linear

Population changes tend to be so slow that we cannot notice them in our daily lives. They include:

- absolute sizes of different groups (e.g. people over 65 or over 85);
- what it means to belong to a group (e.g. single parent), materially or in social terms;
- relationships of groups to each other at a given point (e.g. fathers to children);
- trajectories which individuals follow in moving from one group to another (e.g. from youth to adult).

The next sections give selected factual detail on some of these changes. There are so many aspects that we need a simple framework for thinking about them. For me (as an adult educator, not a demographer) the framework is the distribution of time and opportunity over the lifecourse. The basic sequence education–work–leisure, through which almost all of the population passes, has changed at some points, but at a general level remains remarkably persistent.

We have an *extension* of the first and third phases, and an *intensification* of the second phase. Overall, this is not the optimal way of organising time, for individuals, families or society more broadly.

- Transition from the first phase is longer, more complex and more diverse than before, with a variety of internal sequences. The components of these – finishing education, first job, leaving home, getting married, having children – are now permutable in almost any order, but the effect in many cases has been to prolong young people's dependency.
- The second phase now encompasses both sexes as it used not to. Men work for fewer years than in previous generations, but for longer during the week than elsewhere in Europe. Women work more years and more hours; they have greatly increased their economic activity, largely uncompensated by diminution of unpaid work. This intensification has major implications for family time.
- The third phase is on average hugely extended at both ends, because of earlier labour market exit and particularly increased longevity. It is so long and so populated that it is increasingly strange to define it implicitly in terms of the second phase, as 'retirement' from work. Is the leisure bonanza benefiting us as much as it might?
- We also have a *blurring* of the transitions between phases, both entry into adulthood and the passage from employment. Ambiguity is not necessarily a bad thing. The key overarching question is how adequately these changes are anticipated and influenced by public policy.

Trends and projections

An 'ageing' society

Almost all industrialised countries are ageing. The population of the EU ages by 2.5 months each year, or two years each decade, and its mean age is projected to rise from about 39 to 45 years by 2030 (Lutz, 1999).

Mean age has the advantage of being a single measure, but is obviously limited in the information it provides (notably in respect of variances, e.g. around class, gender or ethnic differences). Interest in – or concern about – an ageing population generally focuses on the elderly or old. But this has dangers:

- it ignores the way generations are interrelated;
- it downplays ageing as a process over the individual lifecourse;
- it involves choices about what counts as 'old' which can be misleading.

What generally drives the measurement is the equation of entry into elderliness with starting to receive a state pension – generally at age 60 or 65. This is how the welfare system and society more broadly draws the line, but the practice looks increasingly outmoded. Accepting it for the time being, Table 1 shows the trend over the last decade and projections for the next four. It shows the UK's position changing significantly, with a much more gradual upward trajectory than in other countries:

Table 1: People over 60 in selected advanced countries, as a percentage of the total population

	1990	2000	2010[a]	2020[a]	2030[a]	2040[a]
France	18.9	20.2	23.1	26.8	30.1	31.2
Germany	20.3	23.7	26.5	30.3	35.3	32.5
Italy	20.6	24.2	27.4	30.6	35.9	36.5
Japan	17.3	22.7	29.0	31.4	33.0	34.4
UK	20.8	20.7	23.0	25.5	29.6	29.5
US	16.6	16.5	19.2	24.5	28.2	28.9

[a] Projections

Sources: Merrill Lynch; Watson Wyatt (FT Survey 10/11/00)

Using 60 as the transition point, an '*old-age dependency ratio*' is calculated by dividing the over-60 population figure by the 20–60 population figure:

- In the EU this ratio is set to rise from 38 per cent to 50 per cent by 2018: whereas currently each pensioner has about three people of working age to support her/him, in under 20 years this will have dropped to two.
- The longer-term projection is that the ratio will rise to over 70 per cent by 2040.

● The ratio is significantly lower for the UK than for most other EU countries (Lutz, 1999).

All Our Futures (BGOP, 2000) summarises trends in the *balance between older and younger people* in the UK:

● In 1900 1 in 25 of the population (4 per cent) was aged 60-plus;
● In 2000 1 in 5 of the population (20 per cent) was aged 60-plus;
● In 2020 1 in 4 of the population (25 per cent) is anticipated to be 60-plus;
● In 1961 25 per cent of the population were under 16;
● In 1994 20 per cent of the population were under 16;
● In 2031 less than 18 per cent of the population are anticipated to be under 16.

By 2008 the *number of pensioners* will have grown to 11.5 million (compared to 10.5 million now) and will exceed the number of children under 16. The increase in the numbers of pensioners will be slowed by the phasing-in of retirement for women between 2010 and 2020, but will rapidly gather pace subsequently. By 2021 there will be 12.2 million pensioners, nearly 20 per cent of the population, and by 2040 this will have risen to 25 per cent (16 million pensioners), with barely half the population under 45 (BGOP, 2000).

But we need also to *differentiate within the category of 'older' people*. As the decades pass, the numbers of 75-year-olds and then 85-year-olds will rise steeply. A more accurate picture of dependency takes into account these shifts *within* the older population (though an exclusive reliance on chronological age will still be misleading). It is here that health issues become extremely significant, with emotional and financial costs which can rise very steeply, for the individual and the family. The numbers are still low.

Table 2: Growth in numbers of people over 65 (1994 to 2031), and numbers and percentages of the UK population over 75 years and 85 years.

Age	1994	2001	2011	2021	2031
All 65-plus (millions)	9.2	9.3	10.0	11.7	14.0
Percentage of population	**15.7**	**15.5**	**16.4**	**19.2**	**23.2**
All 75-plus (millions)	4.0	4.4	4.5	5.2	6.4
Percentage of population	**7.0**	**7.4**	**7.5**	**8.5**	**10.6**
All 85-plus (millions)	1.0	1.2	1.3	1.4	1.8
Percentage of population	**1.7**	**2.0**	**2.1**	**2.3**	**2.9**

Source: BGOP, 2000, Chapter 1.

The forces behind these trends include:

- *Fertility rates* dropped from 91 live births per 1000 women in 1961 to 54 in 2002 (Mathieson and Summerfield, 2000, *Social Trends 34: 2004 edition*, Table 2.16). Constraints on having children include biology (despite technological advances), time, money, social attitudes (e.g. more acceptance of childlessness) and security (psychological as well as material). Fertility rates are not very susceptible to public policy – cf. the ineffectiveness of France's strong pronatalist policies (Ditch, 2000).

- *Mortality rates* have dropped over decades since the 1960s for babies and children and more recently for older people, especially men. Overall mortality rates have dropped from 12.6 per thousand (men) and 11.4 (women) in 1961 to 10.0 and 10.5 in 2002, with projected rates for 2021 of 10.7 and 9.7 (*Social Trends 34: 2004 edition*, Table 1.9). However, the relationship between mortality and morbidity is crucial for the quality of life involved. There are still major class differences in mortality rates.

- *Migration* can counterbalance or outweigh these 'natural' changes: in the 1990s net inward migration in the EU was responsible for more than twice the growth in population due to births over deaths, and somewhat reduced the ageing of the population (*Social Trends 30: 2000 edition*, Table 1.17).

Doing things at a later age

Increased longevity, the growth in the numbers of old people and the rise in mean and median population ages makes 'population ageing' obvious in one sense, that of chronological age. But there are other senses in which it is less obvious, in particular the raising of the age at which various transitions occur.

Biologically young people become adult earlier than before, as the age of puberty declines. However, entry into adulthood as *socially defined* is increasingly deferred:

- Initial education is prolonged. The proportion of 16–18-year-olds in full-time education rose from 35 per cent in 1988 to 55 per cent in 1998 (*Social Trends 30: 2000 edition*, p. 55).

- The average age for entering the labour market rises.

- More young people are financially dependent on their parents for longer.

- Young people take longer to set up independent home: 56 per cent of men and 37 per cent of women aged 20–24 were living with their parents in 2003, compared with 52 per cent and 31 per cent respectively in 1977/8 (*Social Trends 30: 2000 edition*, Table 2.23 and *Social Trends 34: 2004 edition*, Table 2.9).

Other transitions are also being delayed, for example:

- Fewer teenage girls gave birth: the figure fell from 87,000 in 1966 to 46,000 in 1997. (However, this latter figure still represents by far the highest proportion in Europe: the UK rate in 2004 was 29 live births per 1000 girls aged 15–19; in Sweden and Italy the rate was 7 per 1000: *Social Trends 30: 2000 edition*, p. 42; *Social Trends 34: 2004 edition*, p. 35)
- The average age at first marriage increased between 1971 and 2001, from 24.6 to 30.6 years for men, and from 22.6 to 28.4 for women (*Social Trends 34: 2004 edition*, p. 31).
- First childbirths are being delayed. Average age at birth for first child has risen for EU women from 24 in 1970 to 26 in 1995; the median age of childbearing in England and Wales had risen to 28.4 by 1995 (Harper, 2001).

Factors influencing these trends include:

- changes in the *labour market*, with declining demand for young people, especially males with no qualifications, and fewer structured career opportunities from a young age;
- greater autonomy for younger *women*, with higher career aspirations and steeply rising educational achievement;
- decline in availability of what is considered to be *appropriate housing*, linked to rising consumerism and higher aspirations;
- *cyclical* patterns of weaker economic opportunities for some young cohorts, getting them off to a very shaky occupational start;
- *polarisation of life-chances*, notably in the significance of early motherhood.

On the other hand, and paradoxically, the age of official or de facto retirement dropped sharply for men in the 1980s, despite generally better health and longer life expectancy. In 1979, 79.4 per cent of men aged 55–65 were employed; by 1997 this had dropped to 58.3 per cent. For women aged 55–60 the figures are 50.9 per cent and 50.4 per cent (Campbell, 1999). There has recently been a slight upturn in the economic activity rates of older people (NIACE, 2004, Figures 25 and 26), but in general the labour market position of older people remains precarious, despite their higher loyalty and the loss of corporate knowledge involved.

The factors behind this lowering of labour market exit age include:

- cultural attitudes: prejudice about the capacities of older people;
- availability of occupational pensions and 'handshakes';
- desire by older people to retire 'before it's too late';
- government policies, often to disguise unemployment levels;
- low labour demand, especially in certain regions and sectors;
- technological change, perceived and actual, with restricted opportunities for training.

It is hard to disentangle push from pull factors – where decisions are made by the individual (as opposed to imposed on them) it will generally be a combination of them. A major step has already been taken with the raising of women's retirement age. But what will happen to older males, especially those in the current generation, still largely accustomed to lifetime full-time occupations, and many of them with low qualifications?

These trends point in opposite directions, but combine to *condense* the average duration of paid employment for males. It leaves more decades of post-employment leisure. This makes it even more significant that the proportion of retired people participating in learning *fell* over the last seven years, from 20 per cent to 15 per cent (Aldridge and Tuckett, 2004). This is compounded by the significant cohort effect in educational levels. Older people have missed out on the post-war and more recent expansion of educational opportunity; they have less experience of education. This combines with less access to training at work. Twenty-four per cent of 50–59-year-olds last received training 30 or more years ago (Platman, 1999).

Leisure, paid work and learning are not matched up.

Looser families[2]

The *shape* of family structures is changing, becoming longer and thinner – a verticalisation, or move towards the beanpole family, with more generations (because of greater longevity) each with fewer members (fewer children per woman). Fewer children are being born, and family sizes are smaller. This section focuses on the trends which shape the size of families and households, and the relations within them.

It is important to look at family structures in a lifecycle context. Appendix 1 shows the distribution of families across ten discrete types, from 'Young singles' to 'Pensioner couples'. However, family structures are fluid. In assessing trends and their impact we need to bear in mind differences which are due to *cohort effects*.

The current cohort of older adults, aged 60 to 90, were establishing their family lives at a time of low marital dissolution, relatively early age of marriage and birth of first child. The current cohort of young and midlife adults are experiencing relatively high levels of divorce, late age of marriage and first childbirth and periods of extended cohabitation. (Harper, 2001).

---

2   The factual demographic content of this section owes much to Dr Sarah Harper, in particular her book *The Family Within Ageing Societies* (OUP, 2001). Except where otherwise indicated, the figures are from this source.

One major imponderable is how such different experiences of family life will affect intergenerational relations in the future.

The key features of the current position are as following:

Partnership patterns

- British marriage rates are falling by about 3–4 per cent per year.
- *The General Household Survey* suggests a fivefold increase in cohabitation between 1979 and 1995. By 2016 it is projected that there will be more entries into cohabitation than marriages, with unwed births rising to 50 per cent of all births, a milestone that has already been passed in the north east (51 per cent of births were outside of marriage in 2001) (*Social Trends 34: 2004 edition*, p. 34).
- The length of cohabitation is increasing, rising by 70 per cent in the 1980s and 1990s to 34 months in 1995.
- Divorce rates have risen in most Western countries over the last three decades. This rise appears to have been steepest in the 1970s, and has since plateaued. However, the effect on older cohorts is yet to peak: the per cent of people aged 65 or older who are divorced has risen from 1 per cent in 1971 to 5 per cent in 2001, and will reach 12 per cent for men and 13 per cent for women in 2021 (*Social Trends 34: 2004 edition*, Table A3).
- England and Wales have the highest crude (divorces to population) and total (mean number of divorces per 100 marriages) divorce rates in Europe, with around 40 per cent of marriages currently ending in divorce.
- Rates of remarriage, following divorce or widowhood, are also falling. In the last 30 years they have dropped by 75 per cent for men, and over 50 per cent for women.

The rise in divorce has substantial impacts:

- For younger cohorts, men's economic situation appears to improve after divorce, but women's to decline. For those divorced in later life, both sexes experience a decline in their financial position.
- Divorced people have higher mortality rates and worse health.
- Divorce can lead to loneliness and social isolation. Men in particular lose their social networks.
- Interaction between fathers and their children declines after divorce. In 1991 an estimated 750,000 fathers in England and Wales had lost contact with their children following divorce (Wicks, 1995).
- Both manual and non-manual workers' children involved in divorce or separation are more likely to leave school with no qualifications and to have fewer A levels (Wasoff and Dey, 2000).

Lone parenting

- In 1971, 7 per cent of families with dependent children were lone-mother families; by Spring 2003 this had trebled to 23 per cent (*Social Trends 34: 2004 edition*, p. 27).

- In the nineteenth century, lone parenthood was common, resulting from widowhood. In modern times, up to the mid 1980s most of the rise in single parenthood was due to divorce; since then, single lone motherhood (never-married, non-cohabiting women with children) has grown at a faster rate (*Social Trends 30: 2000 edition*, p. 37).

- Lone parenting spans the decades. About two in five lone parents are aged 30–39, and another fifth are aged 40–49 (Rowlinson *et al.,* 1999).

- There is considerable variation by ethnic group. Families from South Asia are very likely to be multi-generational, and to live in multi-generational households. By contrast, a relatively high proportion of households headed by a black ethnic minority member are lone parent families living on their own (*Social Trends 34: 2004 edition*, p. 28).

- The UK is the exception to rule that European countries, unlike the US, have either contained the trend to more teenage lone parent births, or contained its negative social effects (Lesthaeghe, 2000).

The causes and consequences of lone parenting are highly contentious areas. The largest negative characteristic of lone parenting is poverty. Related effects include low labour market participation, and low educational achievement by children: 40 per cent of lone mothers in Britain are in employment (16 per cent full-time), compared with 58 per cent in Germany (35 per cent full-time) and 87 per cent in Sweden (33 per cent full-time) (Wasoff and Dey, 2000). Sixty-nine per cent of their income comes from state benefits (Rowlinson *et al.*, 1999).

Stepfamilies

The corollary of the rise in divorce and remarriage/repartnering has been a growth in stepfamilies. It is estimated that about one in eight children experience life in stepfamilies by the age of 16.

Stepfamilies are more polarised than biological families in relation to time and money: 9 per cent have neither parent in employment, compared with 4 per cent; but they also have a higher proportion with both adults in the labour force (27 per cent compared with 17 per cent). They have lower-than-average household incomes (Ferri and Smith, 1998).

Parental working hours

Although male lifetime working hours have decreased greatly over the last century (roughly from 180,000 to 80,000), that has been largely due to fewer decades in employment. Increased female economic participation, now sustained for more years and with shorter breaks for child-rearing, has increased weekly family working hours greatly. The asymmetry of overall household working time means that women's total working hours have gone up more than men's.

- For full-time employees, both British men and women work longer weeks than any of their European counterparts: 45.2 hours for men and 40.7 for women, compared with European averages of 41.2 and 39.0 (*Social Trends 31: 2001 edition*, Table 4.18). Average weekly hours for all employees are estimated at 44.8 for men and 34.1 for women. Four million regularly work over 48 hours weekly; one in eight work both Saturday and Sunday (Hogarth *et al.*, 2000).

- The increase in female economic activity has largely been due to greater participation by married or cohabiting women (Wasoff and Dey, 2000). In 2003, 63 per cent of single women were in employment, 40 per cent full-time, and 74 per cent of married or cohabiting women were in employment, also 40 per cent full time (*Social Trends 34: 2004 edition*, Table 4.5).

- By 1995, 60 per cent of all women with dependent children were in employment, 22 per cent full-time (Wasoff and Dey, 2000).

- In 1997, 52 per cent of couples with pre-school children were both working, rising to 74 per cent for couples whose youngest child was ten or older (Burghes *et al.*, 1997).

- Mothers in general are returning to work more quickly after childbirth. Four decades ago unqualified women returned to work more quickly than highly qualified women; that pattern is now reversed (Joshi and Paci, 1998).

The *'lifecycle squeeze'* was a term coined in the 1970s. It referred primarily to material factors, with expenses such as children and mortgages crowding in on the (usually sole) breadwinner. Now the squeeze is as much about time, with dual earners increasing many households' wealth but at the expense of family time.

Secondly, the *distribution of working time* across families is very uneven. This affects many aspects, including health. So the squeeze is accompanied by polarisation. One estimate suggests that 2,500 lives might be saved if employment was more equally distributed – and this applied only to those under 65 (Mitchell *et al.*, 2000).

Intergenerational patterns

Changes in the nature and quality of intergenerational relations are hard to assess. They involve social contact and caring, and income and capital allocations. They include education: cohort studies show that parental interest and involvement in children's learning is a crucial factor in educational achievement and subsequent life-chances, generating growing interest in family learning initiatives (Haggart, 2000; Lochrie, 2004).

Increased longevity means that more people are now part of multi-generational families. Other important features include longer intergenerational spacings and growing voluntary childlessness, which both impact upon the nature of intergenerational relations.

- About 75 per cent of respondents in a 1999 survey were part of a three-, four- or five-generation family (Dench *et al.*, 1999). This varies by age: only 19 per cent of middle-aged women (55–63) in the UK had both surviving parent and child (Grundy *et al.*, 1999).
- Intergenerational exchanges of help are fairly common. Most mothers with children under 18 receive help from their mothers, and half of mothers aged 50 and over receive some help from their eldest child.
- Mothers interact more than fathers with children and families, and are less likely to lose contact altogether (*Social Trends 30: 2000 edition*, p. 47).

However, *British Social Attitudes* surveys show a general decline in familial contacts between 1986 and 1995, across all the categories listed (mother, father, sibling, adult child, best friend).

Grandparents exist in increasing numbers. In an ageing society being a grandparent is very important to those who occupy this role, and to other family members:

- Three-quarters of grandparents have often had to put themselves out to look after grandchildren.
- Thirty-four per cent of children under 15 whose mothers are in employment are looked after by a grandparent (*Social Trends 34: 2004 edition*, Table 8. 15).
- Forty-three per cent of those with a grandchild aged 0–5 and 32 per cent with one aged 6–15 see them at least several times a week.
- Conversely, grandchildren also help grandparents; for example, 42 per cent of grandchildren aged 6–15 help their grandparents with household jobs (Dench *et al.*, 1999).

Grandparents also suffer, often in powerlessness, when they lose contact with their grandchildren as a consequence of their children's divorce. On the other hand they may also provide important continuity, support, love and care.

Caring is a major familial function (though not confined to the family).

- Of the UK's 6 million carers, about half are aged 45–64 and nearly 60 per cent are women (*Social Trends 34: 2004 edition*, Table 8. 3).
- A quarter of women aged 51–65 are carers (Foresight Ageing Population Panel, 2000).
- Men figure almost as much as women as carers, but the nature of the caring differs. Male carers tend more to be looking after spouses, women after children or parents (-in-law). Twice as many women as men look after older parents (Cabinet Office, 2000).
- One in six employees have 'eldercare' responsibilities (Kodz *et al.*, 1999).

The combination of these facts points to a growing issue for the labour market. It would be very easy to allow the pressures on these older carers to squeeze them permanently out of the labour market, often at severe personal cost. Twenty-one per cent of the detached male workforce aged 55–64 described themselves as full-time carers (Beatty and Fothergill, 1999a).

Single-person households

- The proportion of single-person households has trebled, from about one in eight in 1961 to around three in ten in 2003 (*Social Trends 34: 2004 edition*, Table 2.2). About one in ten people live on their own. Many of these are older people, but the lifecycle group typology above shows that single people aged 35–64 make up 12 per cent of families; they have below-average income and wealth, and poor pension prospects.

- Many people choose to live alone, and many of these have good social contacts. Solo living is here to stay (44 per cent of women and 22 per cent of men aged 65 or over live alone, and these proportions increase with advancing age (*Social Trends 34: 2004 edition*, Table A5)). However, it may mean increased social isolation. Many of the older people spend much of their time watching television – viewing has gone up to an average of 38 hours per week for older people (*Social Trends 30: 2000 edition*, Table 13.4). Television soaks up solitary time; it may also erode actual or potential social connection.

- There is a high correlation between social connectedness and levels of mental and physical health and wellbeing: 'Statistically speaking, the evidence for the health consequences of social connectedness is as strong today as was the evidence for the health consequences of smoking at the time of the first surgeon general's report.' (Putnam, 2000).

There is a more general debate about the levels of social connectedness which goes well beyond even the broad themes of this paper. Putnam's work on social capital is one of the most widely discussed pieces of social science in the last few decades. He argues that there has been a major long-term but not irreversible decline in social connectedness in the US. Evidence in the UK is more mixed: some components of social capital have declined, others have persisted or grown (Hall, 1999; *Social Trends 33: 2003 edition*, pp. 19–27).

Time has always been in short supply for most people. But changes in family and employment structures pose new challenges if social capital is to be maintained.

Blurred transitions: dependency and ambiguity

'Adulthood'

The different stages in life are rarely clearcut. Philip Aries sparked a debate about how 'childhood' was seen historically. Stanley Hall coined the term 'adolescence' (and later tried to do the same with 'senescence', less successfully).

The prolongation of the period before people attain full independent adult status means that one might speak of the infantilisation of youth. However, it would be more accurate to point to the confusion and ambiguities which surround this transition. Public policy is highly inconsistent in the way it implicitly or explicitly defines this, across a number of policy areas: in education and training, social security, housing and transport, young people are regarded as independent adults at different ages. Appendix 2 spells this out in some detail.

Ambiguity is not necessarily a bad thing, and it would be wrong to have a single rigid chronological age as the threshold. But there are challenges associated with enabling young people to make the transition to adulthood, to recognise this themselves and to have it recognised socially.

'Age' and dependency

The projections on age are presumably as robust as they can be, short of catastrophic changes (not to be excluded – consider the impact of Aids in Africa). The projections on pensions depend on more challengeable assumptions, notably as to what counts as a 'pensioner'. When in the 19th century Bismarck established a public retirement system in Germany, with 70 as the retirement age, life expectancy both there and in the United States was 42. A modern retirement age that bore the same proportionate relation to life expectancy would be 122. Even if the proportion were calculated on the basis of the life expectancy ratio at age 20, the retirement age would be 93. In 1940, a 20-year-old's expectation of retirement was 4 years, or 7 per cent of their adult life. By 1950 this had increased to 12 per cent, and by 1980 to 23 per cent. Even this striking increase is based on official retirement age, and ignores the de facto decrease in the age at which labour market exit occurs; this would bring the figure closer to 40 per cent.[3]

It is the impact of pensions on public expenditure, and to a lesser extent on finance generally, which underlies much of the concern and gives rise to 'demographic timebomb' headlines (OECD, 1999). Assuming current pension systems are maintained, the OECD forecast in 1996 was that most EU member states will be spending 14 per cent or more of GDP on public pensions by 2030. Table 3 gives more detail:

---

3 Instead of determining a given chronological age as retirement age, Boyle Terry suggests that the decennial census could be used to calculate the retirement age to be effective 25 years hence, on the basis of life expectancy changes. For example, normal retirement age might be fixed as the age at which life expectancy is 25 per cent of life expectancy at age 20. Such a formula would have meant that the 1940 age of 65 would have been raised to 66 in 1965, to 67 in 1975 and to 68 in 1995. The lags are sufficient to allow individuals and institutions (employing organisations and pensions institutions) time to adjust – as well as for policy debate to be properly developed in the meantime.

Table 3: Public pension expenditure in the different OECD countries as a percentage of GDP (in 1994 prices)

	1995	2020[a]	2040[a]	2070[a]
Denmark	6.8	9.3	11.6	11.7
Finland	10.1	15.2	18.0	17.8
France	10.6	11.6	14.3	14.0
Germany	11.1	12.3	18.4	15.5
Ireland	3.6	2.7	2.9	2.2
Netherlands	6.0	8.4	12.1	11.0
Spain	10.0	11.3	16.8	16.0
Sweden	11.8	13.9	14.9	15.1
UK	4.5	5.1	5.0	3.1
US	4.1	5.2	7.1	7.4
Japan	6.6	12.4	14.9	14.4

[a] Projections

Sources: Merrill Lynch; Watson Wyatt (FT Survey 10/11/00)

It leaps out from this table that the UK (along with Ireland) is in a very different position to most other countries. This is hugely to the detriment of current UK pensioners. A 2001 international comparison of pensioners' incomes relative to the rest of the population showed relative income to be lower in Britain than in all the countries examined except Australia (Disney and Johnson, 2001). However, this offers correspondingly large opportunities for managing the future. In particular it allows real consideration of the best mix between raising individual or household pensioner incomes and improving infrastructure and services to make the later years of people's lives comfortable and fulfilling. In other words, the debate should not only be about the *level of pensions*; nor just about the *total incomes* of pensioners, from pensions, paid work, investment and other sources (the 'four pillars'); but about the kinds of *enabling services and infrastructures* (formal and informal) which might allow older people to lead fulfilling lives – to 'walk in public without shame', as Adam Smith put it. For example, 0.01 per cent of the annual revenues of occupational pension funds would yield more than enough to transform the learning opportunities and educational services available to older people – including in their pre-retirement phase.

Gender convergence and divergence

In some important respects there has been a convergence in the positions of men and women. Women's economic activity rates come close to men's, and it is projected that more than half the workforce will be female by 2020 (Foresight Ageing Population Panel, 2000). Sometimes the direction is the other way, with male patterns converging towards the female (cf. the drop in older men's activity rates (Young and Schuller, 1990)).

In other respects, divergence continues, for example in longevity. And the trajectories of convergence may, if extended, turn into a new form of divergence. Female achievements in education have now overtaken male at most levels, and the emerging gap is expected to widen. Other divisions remain more or less as they were. So the question of the extent to which we can expect or plan for greater gender symmetry remains unsure.

Future challenges

Some new vocabulary

We may or may not be prisoners of defunct economists, but we are at least partially prisoners of outdated terminology. Should we retain a 'retirement age'? Is 'old age pensioner' a useful way of defining a whole class of people covering 40 or more years? How far are current notions of dependency and dependency ratios constraining rather than aiding social attitudes and policy thinking?
This in turn raises issues of how to divide up this new phase of life after work. The notion of a Fourth Age has been mooted, to be distinguished by its physical dependency from an active Third Age, but has also been criticised for stigmatisation (Laslett, 1988). Perhaps above all we need to address the definition of death, with its set of medical, moral and social issues.

Risk, security and responsibility: assets and benefits

- There is evidence that to have personal assets of even a very modest level is associated with all kinds of better life-chances. It gives both material and psychological security, which enables people to take more control of their lives. How might this kind of positive platform be provided throughout the lifecycle?
- Fear of loss of benefits is closely related: at younger ages fear of losing Housing Benefit inhibits participation in training, and for many older people fear of losing incapacity benefits constrains them from re-entering the labour market (Beatty and Fothergill, 1999b). The integration of social security with labour market and social policies remains a tough challenge. It needs to take full account of the significance of psychological feelings of security and the impact on individuals' perception of risk and reward.
- A 'flexipot' concept would allow individuals to alternate saving and drawing-down to meet mixes of employment, learning and leisure throughout life. The goal should be to achieve a proper balance between risk, security and responsibility. Housing and pension wealth are increasingly important as assets, and highly polarised. They offer great potential for enabling fulfilling use of time, but also for social and familial divisiveness and friction.

Collective funds: using them creatively

At present, colossal amounts of money are saved through pension funds. These rose in the OECD area from 29 per cent of GDP in 1987 to 38 per cent in 1996, but in the UK from 62 per cent to 75 per cent (Blommestein, 1998) – though the fall in equity values in 2000–2001 has resulted in a slight decline, to 71 per cent of GDP as at 31 December 2003 (UBS, 2004). These funds are geared to providing for pensioners' income, which is fundamental; but no attention is paid as to what the impact is or might be beyond this, e.g. by devoting a fraction of the annual revenues for example to:

● improving access to opportunities for learning or civic activities;

● preparation for an active old age; or

● improved transport in order to allow precious contact with (grand)children to be maintained.

There is a twofold challenge:

● to define benefits from the funds' investments in terms of social inclusion as well as material consumption;

● to spread the benefits of these massive funds more effectively over the lifecourse.

Service delivery

Personal services, in the shape of childcare and eldercare, make up a growing market. (Many people will be both providers and consumers of these services.) Employment in it tends to be heavily gendered, poorly paid, low skilled and poorly qualified, with no career structure – sitting very uncomfortably with the ideology of care (Christopherson, 1997). The challenges here are:

● to raise skill and quality levels without unnecessary professionalisation;

● to reconcile paid and unpaid contributions;

● to integrate public, voluntary and private sector delivery;

● to use technologies effectively to give information and access;

● to provide services which enable and do not create unnecessary dependency.

Trust and reciprocation

Family and intergenerational obligations and relationships are certainly put under pressure by the changes described above. There is already considerable uncertainty and often friction, for instance within families over caring responsibilities and bequests, or about commitments to pensions. It would be disastrous if we sped down the road to highly legalistic and zero- or negative-sum sets of arrangements. Trust is a preferable basis, but depends on a transparent and equitable regulatory framework, for institutions, and supportive and sensitive mechanisms for promoting mutuality in complex family situations. Enabling people to avoid or preempt disputes, for example over custody or caring arrangements, and helping them to solve them constructively if they occur, is a major challenge.

Time distribution

The basic argument of this paper is that we need a more rational distribution of time in all the different phases of the lifecourse, with a better balance in each case between paid and unpaid work, leisure and learning (Midwinter, 2000). Younger people need access to opportunities to combine learning with responsibility, to avoid excessive dependency and improve motivation. Further prolongation of formal initial education will not resolve this. Creative packages of reward structures and working conditions are required, in particular to motivate and retain older workers, and to allow employees of all ages to carry out familial and civic responsibilities. Innovative initiatives such as time banks need to be developed, locally or nationally, to build and sustain social capital.

Concluding note

I generally find forced polarities unhelpful. But we can either set as a general goal ever-increasing consumption as a compensation for hectic present or past lives, with real but diminishing returns and probably environmental damage; or a reshaping of opportunity and a better spread of time, to allow learning, social connectedness and participation throughout the lifecourse.

Appendix 1: Gilly–Enis lifecycle groups

Short title	Explanation	Percentage of families in British population	Sample size in the Family Resources Surveys, 1995/6
Young singles	People aged 16–35 not married or cohabiting	17.2	5260
Older singles	People aged 35–64 not married or cohabiting	12.2	3817
Young childless couples	Couples aged 16–35 with no dependent children	4.2	1306
Lone parents	Lone parents with dependent children	6.5	2029
Young couples, young children	Couples with women aged under 35 and pre-school children (aged under 6)	7.4	2300
Older couples, young children	Couples with women aged 35 or more and pre-school children (aged under 6)	2.8	860
Couples, school-age children	Couples with school-age children – child aged six or more	10.5	3258
Older childless couples	Couples aged 35 to 64 with no dependent children	15.1	4661
Pensioner couples	Couples aged 65-plus	9.6	2968
Single pensioners	People aged 65-plus not married or cohabiting	14.5	4568

Source: 1995/96 Family Resources Survey (reproduced from Rowlinson et al., 1999)

Appendix 2: Status ambiguities

Dependence	Independence
Post-16 education and training	
The means-testing of Education Maintenance Allowances assumes dependence on parents	
Training allowance and EMA exclude housing costs and assume dependence on parents.	EMAs will be paid direct to young people.
	Training allowances are not means-tested.
Workers	
Minimum Wage Legislation treats young people (under 22) as dependent or semi-dependent on their parents.	
	Employment protection has been removed from young people, treating them as adults rather than children (i.e. not vulnerable).
Welfare	
16/17-year-olds are excluded from benefit on the basis that they are dependent on their parents, some of whom may receive benefit for them.	
18- to 24-year-olds are on lower rates than adults on the basis that they can be semi-dependent on their parents, who receive no benefit for them.	16/17-year-olds can pay into the NI system, but cannot benefit from it until 18 years of age.
	18- to 24-year-olds contract, as adults, to seek work under the Jobseeker's Allowance, New Deal, etc.
Higher education	
In assessing tuition fees payable, the government treats students as dependents (means-testing their parents or spouse). The student is required to depend on his/her parents or spouse to pay tuition fees.	
	Student loans. The student is personally liable for repayment, which is based on his/her income only. The student both enters a contract with a lender and begins repayments as an independent adult.
Housing and transport	
Subsidised transport treats those in education as dependent If they were living with their parents, the family could be housed because it contains dependent children.	Subsidised transport treats those in training as adults.
Young people are deemed in social security terms able to live with their parents.	Young people are only entitled to local authority housing if they are perceived as vulnerable, and age is not usually a criterion of vulnerability – i.e. they are treated as adults.

Source: Jones, and Bell, 2000.

23

References

Aldridge, F and Tuckett, A (2004) *Business as Usual …? The NIACE Survey on Adult Participation in Learning 2004*, NIACE.

Beatty, C and Fothergill, S (1999a) *The Detached Male Workforce*, cited in *Transitions After 50*.

Beatty, C and Fothergill, S (1999b) *Incapacity Benefit and Unemployment*, p. 7, cited in *Transitions After 50*.

BGOP (2000) *All our Futures*, Report of the Steering Committee of the Better Government for Older People Programme 15/6/00, Chapter 1, p. 6.

Blommestein, H (1998) 'Pension Funds and Financial Markets', *OECD Observer*, p. 212.

Burghes, L, Clarke, L and Cronin, N (1997) *Fathers and Fatherhood in Britain*, Family Policy Studies Centre, p.46.

Bynner, J., Joshi, H. and Tsatsas, M. (1999) *Obstacles and Opportunities on the Route to Adulthood*, Adam Smith Institute.

Cabinet Office (2000) *More Choice for Women in the New Economy*.

Campbell, N (1999) *The Decline of Employment Among Older People in Britain*, LSE, Table 1.

Christopherson, S (1997) *Childcare and Elderly Care: What Occupational Opportunities for Women?* OECD/GD (97) p. 215.

Dench, G *et al.* (1999) 'The role of grandparents', in *British Social Attitudes – the 16th report: Who shares New Labour values?* NCSR.

Disney, R and Johnson, P (2001) *Pension Systems and Retirement Incomes Across OECD Countries*, Edward Elgar

Ditch, J, (2000) *Fee, Fo, Fi, Fum: Fertility, Social Protection and Fiscal Welfare*, paper given at European Observatory on the Social Situation, Demography and Family Annual Seminar 2000: Low Fertility, Families and Public Policies, 15–16 September 2000.

Ferri, E and Smith, K (1998) *Step-parenting in the 1990s*, Joseph Rowntree Foundation/Family Policy Studies Centre.

Foresight Ageing Population Panel (2000), *Labour, Leisure and Learning*, Taskforce Report, Annex 1, p. 9.

Grundy, E, Murphy, M *et al.* (1999) 'Looking beyond the household', in *Population Trends*, 97, 19–27.

Haggart, J. (2000) *Learning Legacies: A Guide to Family Learning*, NIACE

Hall, P (1999) 'Social capital in Britain', *British Journal of Political Science*, 29, 417–61.

Harper, S (2001) *The Family Within Ageing Societies* (OUP, 2001) p. 5.

Hogarth, T *et al.* (2000) *Work–Life Balance 2000: Baseline study of work–life balance practices in Great Britain*, (Summary Report) Institute for Employment Research: Nov 2000, p. 7.

Jones, G. and Bell, R (2000) 'Youth, parenting and public policy, *Balancing Acts: Youth parenting and public policy,* YP5.

Joshi, H and Paci, P (1998) *Unequal Pay for Women and Men: Evidence from the British birth cohort studies*, MIT Press.

Kodz, J, Kersley, B and Bates, B (1999) *The Fifties Revival*, Institute for Employment Studies Report 359, cited in *Transitions After 50*.

Laslett, P (1988) *A Fresh Map of Life*, Weidenfeld and Nicholson.

Lesthaeghe, R (2000) *Europe's Demographic Issues: Fertility, Household Formation and Replacement Migration*, Interuniversity papers in demography, Interface demography (Soco) Vrije Universiteit Brussel, p.23.

Lutz, W (1999) 'Will Europe be Short of Children?', *Family Observer*, 1, 8–16.

Mathieson, J and Summerfield, C (eds), *Social Trends 30: 2000 edition*, London: Office for National Statistics, 2000, Table 2.13.

Midwinter, E (2000) *Towards a Balanced Society: A contextual commentary on the Debate of the Age*, Age Concern.

Mitchell, R, Shaw, M and Dorling D (2000) *Inequalities in Life and Death: What if Britain were more equal?* Joseph Rowntree Foundation/Policy Press.

NIACE (2004) *Adult Learning at a Glance: The UK Context, Facts and Figures 2004*, NIACE.

OECD (1999) *Maintaining Prosperity in an Ageing Society*.

Platman, K (1999) 'Family and Working Lives Survey', in *The Glass Precipice: Employability for a mixed age workplace*, Employers Forum on Age/Age Concern, cited in *Transitions after 50*, New Policy Institute, p.24.

Putnam, R D (2000) *Bowling Alone: The Collapse and Revival of American Community*, Simon and Schuster.

Rowlinson, K, Whyley, C and Warren, T (1999) *Wealth in Britain: A Lifecycle Perspective*, Policy Studies Institute.

Sargant, N (2000) *The Learning Divide Revisited*, NIACE, Table 8.

Social Trends 30: 2000 edition, The Stationery Office: available at http://www.statistics.gov.uk/downloads/theme_social/st30v8.pdf (accessed 21 December 2004).

Social Trends 31: 2001 edition, The Stationery Office: available at http://www.statistics.gov.uk/downloads/theme_social/social_trends31/ST31(final).pdf (accessed 5 January 2005).

Social Trends 32: 2002 edition, The Stationery Office: available at http://www.statistics.gov.uk/downloads/theme_social/Social_Trends32/Social_Trends32.pdf (accessed 5 January 2005).

Social Trends 33: 2003 edition, The Stationery Office: available at http://www.statistics.gov.uk/downloads/theme_social/Social_Trends33/Social_Trends_33.pdf (accessed 5 January 2005).

Social Trends 34: 2004 edition, The Stationery Office: available at http://www.statistics.gov.uk/downloads/theme_social/Social_Trends34/Social_Trends34.pdf (accessed 5 January 2005).

UBS (2004) *International Pension Fund Comparisons*, UBS Global Asset Management: available at http://www.e-fundresearch.com/tmp/UBS+Pension+Funds+2004.pdf (accessed 5 January 2005).

Wasoff, F and Dey, I, (2000) *Family Policy*, Gildredge Press, p. 66.

Wicks, M (1995) quoted in Walker, J, McCarthy, P and Simpson B, 'Renegotiating Fatherhood', in *Being There: Fathers after divorce*, Newcastle Centre for Family Studies, 1995.

Young, M and Schuller, T (1990) *Life After Work*, Harper Collins.

An ageing population: points for an educational response

Key policy aims

1. Provide more learning opportunities for older adults, beginning early (i.e. well before retirement).
   Generally expand volume of existing adult education provision, including training for teachers. This is a particular area for local government to exercise initiative, without the need for national standards.
   Extend guidance services to include customised service for older adults.
   Link provision to mass media, e.g. using BBC website as source of promotion/information about educational opportunities, especially local.
   Promote access to education/educational leave as a standard component of the last year(s) of employment: invite employers to demonstrate best practice.

2. Develop cost/benefit calculations which take into account the full costs of age-related dependency.
   Estimate cost of loss of economic activity through inadequate skills.
   Construct reasonable, modest assumptions about education's potential to reduce/postpone dependency, e.g. x pounds will have a z per cent impact on:
   - health service resources: visits to GP, drugs, bed blocking in hospitals;
   - cost of elder-carers' absence from labour market;
   - weekly residential care costs.
   Estimate non-financial knock-on effects of caring for elders.
   Assess particular impact on gender equality goal.

3. Broaden the pensions mindset, to include quality of life alongside material income.
   Strike a political bargain, with public investment in more generous educational facilities as part of raising of retirement age.
   Open discussions with pension funds as to how their responsibilities might extend to quality of life issues.

4. Make intergenerational cohesion a central component of social cohesion.
   Investigate potential use of grandparents/older people in schools and colleges, as teaching assistants or in other roles.
   Promote family learning which includes grandparents and other members of older generations; e.g. learning ICT skills together; doing family history.
   Explore potential for cross-generational cultural activity, e.g. in creative arts.

2. The age of choice: a new agenda for learning and work?

Stephen McNair, Centre for Research into the Older Workforce, University of Surrey

Debates about the purposes of education are as old as education itself, and commentators continue to argue about the balance between economic, social, cultural and recreational purposes. How far is 'education' distinguishable from 'training', and how far should what is offered, and on what terms, be decided by employers or the State rather than individuals themselves?

Until the last 20 years, older people figured little in these debates. Few people over 50 participated in publicly funded learning, and it was generally assumed that they were marginal to the discussion. Where they appeared at all it was only in relation to explicitly 'recreational' learning (even if, for some, that recreational learning had a fairly academic focus, as in the case of university extramural programmes), the assumption being that learning in age must be related only to non-vocational objectives.

However, in recent years, increasing life expectancy and broader social and economic changes have begun to change this. Larger cohorts are retiring and smaller ones entering the labour market, and skills and labour shortages are beginning to be very evident, especially in the more economically prosperous south of England. As a result, the potential of older people to contribute to the economy has begun to be an issue in policy debate. However, after age 50 the proportion of the population which is economically active drops steadily, and the National Audit Office has estimated the cost of this, in lost earnings and taxes and increased welfare payments, as £20–30 billion p.a. Government is keen to reverse the trend towards earlier retirement[1] and this raises issues both about how individuals can be helped or encouraged to stay longer in the labour market, and how employers might make work more attractive to them.

---

1 Real retirement ages fell steadily through the last quarter of the twentieth century, but there are some signs recently that this has begun to reverse.

It follows that policy-making needs to be better informed about how the older labour market works: about the motivation of older workers and of employers, about the behaviour of both, and the training and educational issues which may arise. This is a relatively unexplored territory, and this chapter aims at least to lay out some parameters for further study and policy.

The age of choice? working and not working

As participants in the labour market, older people are distinctive. For people aged between 20 and 50, paid work is a central and unavoidable feature of life. However, there comes a point, somewhere between the ages of 50 and 60, when staying in employment begins to be a matter of choice, not necessity. The average age of actual retirement for men and women has been converging, and now stands around 62 for both, as more women work later in life (particularly part-time), and many men retire earlier than the State Pension Age.[2] Some 'retire', voluntarily or through ill health, in their early 50s, while others are still seeking new challenges and career opportunities in their late 60s. Very few people retire from paid employment voluntarily before the age of 55, but the overwhelming majority have done so by 65.

During this phase of life, for most people stretching from the late 40s to the mid 60s, engagement with paid employment diminishes. This is a period during which choices are made about work and life retirement on different terms, and under different pressures, from those applying to younger people. Competing alternatives to paid work – caring roles, voluntary work, or leisure activities of varying kinds – begin to be available for many, and eventually most, while pension provision of some kind begins to offer an alternative income. However it is still true that, for most, retirement remains a sometimes painful 'cliff edge' transition from full-time work on Friday to full-time retirement on Monday.

To describe this as the 'age of choice' does not imply that the choices are all on the part of the individual. Some choose, and some are chosen, and the forces which polarise the labour market generally – social class, qualifications and gender – have an even stronger influence on the choices available to those over 50 than on their younger peers.[3] The 'choosers' in general have high qualifications, are in professional and managerial work and have significant savings or pension entitlements. For them the choice lies with the individual, and is between competing attractions: if they find their work interesting, challenging or part of some kind of lifelong mission they are likely to stay, and employers are likely to want to retain them. On the other hand, the 'survivors', generally have no or low qualifications, are in unskilled or semi-skilled work, and have little or no company

---

2 The long-term trend to earlier retirement for men through the last quarter of the twentieth century appears to have reversed recently.

3 Much of the following analysis is based on a major study of job change in the workforce, carried out in 2003 by the Centre for Research into the Older Workforce, with ONS (McNair *et al.*, 2004).

pension entitlement. For them the challenge is to make the compromises necessary to hold on to a job, in the knowledge that returning to the labour market will be increasingly difficult as they grow older.

However, in an economy where skills levels are generally rising, the number of jobs for the unskilled is not growing, and the unskilled are disproportionately represented among those seeking work after 50. Furthermore, for those with low qualifications, health is a major factor. The main reason for 'retirement' before the age of 55 is ill health and disability, concentrated overwhelmingly in those carrying out manual occupations, and retirement on this basis has a major damaging impact on the quality of life after retirement in terms of continuing ill health, low income, social isolation and early death.

This polarisation of the labour market is familiar, although the divide probably deepens as people get older. However, there is a third group, in addition to the 'choosers' and 'survivors' who we have called 'jugglers'. These remain in work, but on a part-time basis, combining paid employment with other roles, most often caring for relatives or other dependents. While for some among this group money is a vital motivation, there is a substantial proportion for whom paid work on a part-time basis is an active choice, not a matter of desperate necessity. Unlike the 'chooser' and 'survivor' groups, where two-thirds are male, 'jugglers' are overwhelmingly women, the proportion of whom in the 50-plus workforce is rising, but alongside them is a much smaller group of men, who 'retire' from high-skill and stressful work into less demanding, sometimes unskilled or manual, occupations or part-time work in order to reduce stress while maintaining social contacts and the sense of being useful to society. These groups may be forerunners of a different kind of workforce, more flexible and with a different approach to work-life balance.

Pressures for change

Three broad factors are currently combining to change the pattern of retirement behaviour. The first is the need of the labour market for more people. The size of the potentially economically active population is falling. The pattern of birth-rates over the last 50 years has resulted in the largest-ever cohorts reaching retirement age, while the birth-rate has fallen to below replacement rate, and there has been a slimming of the middle aged cohort from which much of the managerial workforce has traditionally come. On present trends, by 2021 the UK population will have grown by 1.9 million, but the workforce by less than half that. The OECD has suggested that developed countries will need to double their immigration rates if they are to keep pace with the labour needs implied in current economic growth plans.

Persuading people to stay in work longer may be a less politically contentious means of solving the economic problem. Age Concern has estimated that an annual growth in the proportion of 50–69 year olds in work of only 0.25 per cent would keep the ratio of workers to population stable, generating an increase in national income of £31 billion and raising average UK output per person by £500.

However, the problems are not evenly spread across the workforce. Labour and skills shortages are particularly severe in the south of England and in particular economic sectors, while unemployment remains high in some parts of the north.[4] The government's 2003 Skills Strategy identifies an ageing workforce as a serious constraint on growth in six of the fourteen occupational sectors. A further complicating factor is the impact of historical cycles in the labour market. one of the first responses is to cut back on recruitment and training, sometimes for several years, producing a skewed age profile in the workforce in later years and gaps in the patterns of promotion and succession which can be very disruptive to the business. Such effects can be found in occupations as diverse as nursing, construction, gas-fitting and the police.

The second pressure for change comes from the economic costs of financing a longer period of retirement, for more people. Whether life after retirement is financed by the state or by private pension arrangements, lengthening retirement means either that the resources available to pay for the retired have to be spread more thinly, resulting in increased pensioner poverty, or those in work have to contribute more to maintaining the retired. Neither is politically attractive, and the situation is aggravated by historically low levels of personal savings.

The third factor, of particular importance to education and training, is the issue of meaning and purpose in later life, when retirement is no longer five years of poor health, but 20 or more years of potentially active life contributing to the community. For most people, (especially men, but increasingly women too) paid work is an important part of the sense of personal identity and of social networks. For a small minority, education has always provided a means of re-establishing both meaning in life, and social networks, but this remains very much a minority choice.

The policy response

In response to these pressures, governments throughout the developed world are seeking to extend working life, and the EU has taken the view that age discrimination in the workplace, including compulsory retirement, should be treated as seriously as other forms of unfair discrimination. Gradually the UK government is changing the regulatory frameworks to encourage people to stay in work, by allowing them to phase out of work gradually, and to draw a pension while continuing to work for the same employer.

---

4   In regions and areas where employment opportunities are limited, unemployment itself leads to poor health, at which point 'unemployed' people become 'long-term sick', and are reclassified in government statistics as retired on ill health grounds rather than unemployed.

The same pressures are also producing change in employer behaviour. As skills and labour shortages bite, and full employment for people with some sort of qualification becomes the norm, at least in Southern Britain, employers are beginning to add age discrimination to their equal opportunities policies, and remove age criteria from job descriptions and recruitment procedures. Some are also adopting employment practices which make work more attractive to older people. Flexible working arrangements are becoming more common, including part-time, progressive retirement, seasonal working for those who wish to take extended holidays or spend winters abroad, and carer leave (since many people in their 50s and 60s now have dependent elderly relatives or are caring for grandchildren). However, these are still more common in the largest firms, and concentrated in sectors with particular problems, like construction, health and care. For different reasons, similar strategies are being adopted in retailing and financial services, where the need to staff for longer opening hours calls for a more diverse workforce, and because many large retailers have recognised that an ageing population means ageing customers, many of whom prefer to be served by people who are more like themselves in experience and knowledge.

Some employers have found that the changes they had to make to accommodate legislation on parental leave were not as disruptive as they anticipated, and have extended the same rights to those with caring responsibilities.[5] Some older workers also take up freelance and consultancy work, either as a long term option or as a means to phase gradually out from paid work. However, most of these changes are not evenly distributed across the workforce. Major retailers, for example, are much more likely to offer flexible working into the 70s for checkout operators than for senior managers, where the full-time model still tends to dominate

In understanding long-term patterns it is important to recognise that different generations may have very different expectations of retirement. Those who reached 60 in 1990 were shaped by pre-war attitudes and values. They entered adult life in the aftermath of war and experienced the economic boom of those manufacturing industries which went into terminal decline in the 1980s, taking with them the demand for the industrial skills of their whole generation. Although a minority experienced the unexpected wealth of strong occupational pensions schemes, their expectations of life, and of retirement, were set in the 1950s, when retirement was a brief period, often of ill health, at the end of 40 years of working life. By contrast, those who will reach 60 in 2010 experienced the full effects of post-war educational reforms, and entered adulthood in the very different social and economic climate of the late 1960s. In general, their expectations of life, and their qualifications, are significantly higher. They have far greater ambitions for the twenty-plus years of active retirement than their parents had of their ten or

---

5   As the average lifespan increases a growing proportion of people in their 50s and 60s find themselves caring for elderly relatives.

fewer. They are also more likely to want to work, and to be physically and emotionally capable of doing so. But they are also more likely to want to make choices about this, and for many work is one option among many, to be chosen only if the terms are right in terms of role, autonomy and flexibility.

The implementation of the European Age Discrimination Directive, and the abolition of contractual retirement ages which is eventually likely to accompany it, will be an important step in opening opportunities to older people and addressing some major economic issues, although an opportunity for some may be an imposition on others. However, age is unlike most, if not all, other kinds of discrimination, in that its impact is universal, and does have a foundation in real changes in capacity. Age is something which everyone experiences, and with ageing comes inevitable, albeit often long-delayed, decline in both physical and mental capacities. It may be inappropriate to set a simple retirement date based on chronological age, since different individuals change differently over time, and many 70-year-olds are more capable of work than many 50-year-olds, but there will be cases where employer and employee disagree about an individual's capacity to continue in work, and issues about how much adjustment an employer must make to accommodate changing individual capacity.[6]

Managing this process will not be easy, and it may make significant new demands on human resource professionals and employers more generally. In an ideal world there would be joint career planning from the early 50s onwards designed to maximise the use of the individuals' skills as long as they wished and were capable, and to provide a civilised, probably phased, exit with dignity at an agreed point. In reality most workplaces are not like this. However, there is a moral responsibility on the employer and the state to ensure that this transition is managed well, since there is good research evidence that the quality of an individual's life after retirement is significantly affected by the way he or she leaves work: those whose experience of leaving the workforce is of rejection (sometimes both personal and professional), have poorer health, shorter lives and less social contact (Phillipson, 2002).

Aspirations to work

The National Audit Office estimates that of the 2.7 million people between 50 and state pension age not in work, around one-third would like to work, and about 7 per cent are actively seeking work. However, after the age of 50 it becomes increasingly difficult for anyone unemployed to re-enter the labour market, and the difficulty of doing so increases rapidly with the length of unemployment. Many simply become discouraged and redefine themselves as 'early retired', sick or disabled, rather than 'unemployed'. For those in work, the commitment to work is even stronger. CROW's work on the older labour market found that 80

---

6 This is particularly complex since the Disability Discrimination Act requires employers to make adjustments to accommodate the circumstances of people experiencing a disability.

per cent of those in work over 50 would consider working after 'normal retirement' if the terms were right.

Nevertheless, at some point everyone comes to see themselves as 'approaching retirement' and begins to plan for this. Some do so decades before, while for others it is a matter of days or weeks. This process changes the psychological contract with the employer, and attachment to work itself, and some new factors – financial commitments, caring roles, study, travel, and family – come into play. For a sizable proportion, perhaps a majority, some form of continuing paid work could be attractive. It remains to be seen whether the implementation of age discrimination legislation will result in a larger proportion of this group taking up the opportunity to stay in work, and if so what kind of work and on what terms.

What does this mean for education and training?

The principal feature of vocational learning in later life is depressingly familiar to anyone who has studied adult learning. Those who have had least previous education get least continuing education. Those whose skills and knowledge are least likely to equip them to stay employable are the least likely to receive any training. It seems that many older people and many employers still share the two common prejudices: that 'you can't teach an old dog new tricks' or that investing in older people is a waste of money because the payback period is too short.

Neither of these widely held beliefs has any real foundation. There is little evidence that most people's capacity to learn or work (in most occupations) diminishes significantly with age during the 50s and 60s, provided the individual is sufficiently motivated and trained. Indeed the evidence is clear that most of the decline in capacity which can be identified among older workers is related not to age, but to failure to train and to invest in motivation and job design. People get the message that they are not expected to be there for long, and that their contribution is not valued, and so they work with less commitment. This erosion of the implicit contract and trust between employee and employer is damaging for productivity and for the emotional health of the individual. However, older workers change jobs less frequently than younger ones, so a trained 50 year old is less likely than a 30 year old to take his or her new skills to a new employer, and many workers see such investment by their employer as a sign that they and their work are valued, and they repay this with loyalty.

However, even if this age inequity were to be overcome, the level of identifiable support for learning at work would be unimpressive. The CROW national survey of job change in 2003 found that 40 per cent of workers who changed their jobs said that their new role had either 'required a lot more skills' or involved increased responsibility, but one-third of these had received no support of any kind (training, guidance, advice, books, internet) to take on these new responsibilities, and the evidence suggested that this pattern strengthened with age.

It is possible that the extent of work related learning undertaken by older people is underestimated because much research measures only qualifications, or participation in formal education and training courses which are easy to identify, but are more likely to be pursued by younger people. It may be that older workers are more likely to use informal routes to learning, which are more difficult to track and measure. If this were true, learning would still be happening, but in ways which are not easy to identify, and which the individuals themselves might not describe as learning. This does not necessarily mean that educators should ignore it: rather that they should devote more energy to understanding how to support and facilitate work-based learning.

What is evident, however, is that there is very little explicit provision of education and training opportunities for older workers.[7] What there is, is disproportionately taken up by two relatively small groups of such workers: those with high qualifications and incomes (paid for by employers), and those who are unemployed (paid for by the state).

Do older workers have different learning needs?

If older workers were like younger workers in their behaviour and needs, the policy objective would be simple: to improve their participation rates in education and training, by consciously targeting them for recruitment. However there is little evidence of this happening yet. The National Audit Office found only 7 of the 47 Local Learning and Skills Councils paying any explicit attention to older learners and very little attention being given to the issue by Regional Development Agencies. The government's prioritising of Level 2 qualifications and basic skills has the potential to help with this, but the very strong emphasis of government on the needs of 14–19 year olds runs a risk of intensifying the neglect of the older workforce, and these strategies are unlikely alone to make much impact on the issues of self confidence and self esteem which form a significant barrier to entry to the labour market for many older people.

However, in addition to access to the mainstream of education and training, there are learning needs associated with work which are different for older people, and for which distinct forms of provision are also required. While it is possible (though evidence is scarce), that there are changes in ways of working and learning which relate directly to age itself (perhaps learning styles change with age?), it is much more likely that the changes relate either to cohort effects (relating to previous life experiences of particular generations) or because the approach of the end of paid employment changes motivation and objectives.

---

7 Although there are many small-scale local projects and initiatives.

There is no identifiable point at which people become 'older workers', but there are four distinctive features of work which have a bearing on how education and training strategies should be designed:

- **The central role of employers** Frequency of job change (including change to a new role with the same employer) reduces with age, suggesting that for older workers, skills development is more dependent on their employer than it is for younger workers. Here employers' reluctance to train older workers needs challenging.

- **The importance of 'career' motivation.** The most important motive for job change for most people at least until the late 60s, are 'career' related (new challenges, promotion etc).[8] Creating a sense of career advance, rather than waiting to escape, will raise motivation, and generate developmental learning needs. Approaches to learning which raise self-esteem and confidence, and which renew or replace skills, will contribute to this.

- **The search for flexible working.** A large proportion of people say that they would consider working after 'normal' retirement age if the work could be part-time and flexible. However few appear to do so.

- **Avoiding poor health.** Declining health and the rise of chronic medical conditions is a very significant factor in early exit from the labour market, especially for the low-skilled and those in manual occupations. However, there is interesting evidence from Finland that explicit strategies for reorganising work in the 40s and 50s can reduce the risks of premature retirement on health grounds. Learning to manage one's health better (and helping employers to design less stressful work) is clearly an important equity issue.

The following list indicates some of the kinds of educational provision which might address these issues. Most exist in some form, but none are available on anything like the scale required to address the broad issue of significantly reducing premature exit from the labour market, let alone raising real retirement ages.

- **Advice, guidance and support.** Information, Advice and Guidance services remain uneven in quality and distribution, and little known: further, older people are less likely to take them up than younger ones. However, for people who may not have changed jobs for decades, or for those who are unemployed and with low skills, individual advice, and ongoing support are probably critical to morale, to skills development, and to helping them back into the labour market, as is active brokering of job opportunities and work experience. There are also, of course, commercial and voluntary recruitment and support agencies like PRIME, which have developed a special interest in older workers, actively 'selling' them to employers in terms of established skills, reliability, loyalty, and flexibility.

---

8   The CROW survey found that 30 per cent of all job-changers in their 50s gave career reasons like promotion and new challenges as the motivation for changing their jobs, and this was still a significant factor for people in their 60s.

- **'Lifecourse education'** to help people plan over the long term for the transition to retirement is one obvious priority for older workers. Although professionals in pre-retirement education have always argued that it should not be left to the last weeks before retirement, this has often been the case, and only a very small minority of workers have any access to it, although recent research suggests that most people begin to plan for their retirement several years in advance of when they expect to leave. As we move towards a more flexible and permeable boundary between employment and retirement, learning to plan and manage this major life change becomes increasingly complex. A much expanded pre-retirement curriculum will need to focus on health (including remaining sufficiently healthy to remain in work), finance (where many people make very badly informed decisions with major impact on the rest of their lives), relationships and leisure, but also on employment rights and options, and on the skills of negotiating one's personal retirement path, as well as helping people to manage the social and emotional adjustments of changing status and roles.

- **Updating** is a critical area in a world of rapid technological and social change. In organisations with a relatively young workforce and high levels of staff turnover, induction training may provide the skills needed to keep up, especially if the employer succeeds in recruiting people trained and experienced in other firms, but the need for older workers, who are likely to have been in the firm longer, to keep up may easily be overlooked.

- **Re-entry** is especially important in occupations like nursing, where skills shortages are leading employers to seek ways of persuading those who have retired or left for family or other reasons to return to the workforce. Their original training may be perfectly sound, but they will need not only to refresh their older skills, but also to learn about developments in treatment or technology which have taken place while they were away. This requires something different from simply delivering the same training as is offered to new entrants. This may be particularly important where roles have been redefined as the workforce in general becomes more flexible and multi-skilled, creating real challenges for trainers.

- **Health education**. A major reason for premature withdrawal from the labour market is ill health and disability. Finnish experience suggests that explicit health interventions, including job redesign, for people in their 40s and early 50s can significantly increase the employability of many people in their late 50s and 60s. Helping people to understand the ways in which work damages their health, and helping employers to design work to impose fewer physical and psychological stresses would help with this. So would strategies to encourage employers to review the balance of work across the lifecourse, employing older people on less physically demanding jobs to conserve their skills and knowledge.

- **Education for succession**. A notable feature of the over-65 workforce is the dominance of the self-employed. No doubt this partly reflects the intrinsic motivation which comes from being in control of one's own work and life. However, observers have noted that some such workers appear to find themselves unable, emotionally or practically, to hand over the business. Education to help people to plan for succession might be good both for business and individual.

- **Education for mentoring**. One role which older workers can usefully play is in providing mentoring for younger and less experienced colleagues. This happens informally in many organisations, and some employers are actively developing strategies to promote this. The potential for using the skills of older people in this way is probably underdeveloped, particularly in the numbers of very experienced managers who take early retirement, and whose managerial skills might be very relevant to new businesses, or small firms trying to expand. However, there are issues of adaptation to new contexts, and managing complex emotional relationships with younger entrepreneurs. Education programmes designed to help potential mentors to develop appropriate skills could be good for the businesses supported, and for the self esteem and social engagement of the Mentors.

Finally, it is worth noting that many of the adjustments to attitudes and self image which this paper has discussed are not addressed educationally by formal instruction. Experience of education for unemployed people, for example, has demonstrated that the effectiveness of education at addressing such learning needs depends critically on pedagogy which stresses the development of the individual, of building on past experience and on peer group support. Sometimes *how* teaching happens is as important as what is taught.

Implications for policy and practice

It seems clear that older workers are underrepresented in education and training, and this is probably not economically or socially desirable. If government wishes to intervene to overcome this problem there are a number of key messages:

- **Recognise the diversity of people**. People do not get more alike as they age, and their learning needs are equally various. Initiatives need to recognise the very different experiences of choosers, survivors and jugglers, and of people who have worked in different sectors
- **Address both retention and re-entry**. It is much easier to retain older workers in the workforce than to enable those who have left, for whatever reason, to re-enter. The evidence from initiatives like New Deal 50+ is that re-entry is possible, but requires intensive support, not least to overcome employers' prejudices about older workers. This may change when the Age Discrimination Directive comes into force.
- **Encourage personal autonomy**: a general lesson from adult learning practice, and from recent research is that willingness to stay in work is closely related to the individual's sense of control over his or her work and life. This also impacts on the quality of the work which they do. Initiatives should be designed to enhance, not undermine this, and particularly challenge the prejudices which many older people themselves have about their limitations.

- **Recognise the diversity of firms and sectors**: Firms are not all alike. Employment practices vary greatly according to size and sector. The size of the employing organisation has a bearing on the likelihood of people staying in work, and the quality of that work. Older workers in large firms are more likely to describe their experience of work in positive terms, but in general retire earlier. The self employed are much more likely to be still working in their late 60s and 70s than any other group. Some sectors are more prepared to recruit older workers because of skill gaps and shortages.

References

Age Concern (2004) *The Economy and Older People*, Age Concern Reports.

Cabinet Office (2000) *Winning the Generation Game: Improving Opportunities for People Aged 50–65 in Work and Community Activity*, Cabinet Office.

Controller and Auditor General (2004) *Welfare to Work: Tackling the Barriers to the Employment of Older People*, House of Commons, London.

Ilmarinen, J (2002) *What the social partners can do to improve employment opportunities for older workers*. Keynote speech, 'Improving Employment Opportunities for Older Workers'; Ninth EU-Japan Symposium, Brussels, 21–22 March 2002. Available at: http://europa.eu.int/comm/employment_social/international_cooperation/other_files/eu_japan_symposium9/speech_ilmarinen_en.pdf (accessed 21 December 2004).

McNair, S, Flynn, M, Owen, L, Humphreys, C, and Woodfield, S (2004) *Changing work in later life: a study of job transitions*, University of Surrey.

Phillipson, C (2002) *Transitions from Work to Retirement: Developing a new social contract*, The Policy Press.

Regan, D (2000) *Learning in Later Life: Motivation and Impact*, DFEE.

Department for Education and Skills (2003) *21st Century Skills: realising our potential*, Command 5810.

European Commission (2000) *Council Directive 2000/78/EC*

3. Fit for purposes: do policies and planning work for older learners?

Judith Summers, NIACE Research Fellow

Introduction

If you asked your family, friends and colleagues what being an 'older adult' or 'retired' meant to them, you would probably get very different responses. Some might be worrying about pensions, disposable income, or what happens when they become infirm. Some might want or have to go on in some sort of paid work, others to be involved in the community. Some but not all would look forward to financial ease and activity. Some would think of sociability, others fear loneliness. Some might expect to be carers, some to need care. We are all aware of how the experience of being older is diverse and changing.

What does all this mean for adult learning? What are the challenges?

- Equity: the relationship between higher initial educational achievement, income, quality of life and continuing participation in learning continues to apply for older adults and the learning divide is as powerful in the Third Age as earlier in life.

- Working life: the increasing length of the 'Third Age' of active, independent retirement and the likelihood that people will need or want to stay in paid work for longer each create new learning interests.

- The needs of adults in the 'Fourth Age' of decline and infirmity: to maintain mental and physical activity and quality of life.

- The particularities of age and learning: the ways in which not only social class, but gender, ethnicity, disability, sexuality and location may affect what and how we want to learn, or make barriers.

- Countering marginalisation: learning which connects with opportunities to engage in civil society and helps to overcome the familiar experiences in ageing of isolation or a sense of loss and rootlessness.

This paper is about how far policies, planning and local services reflect these challenges, and is informed by four case studies of how things work in practice. Three LEA Adult and Community Learning (ACL) services in neighbouring but very different areas of the north-west were the main focus, both because of the role of ACL in non-qualification bearing adult learning and because the government's 2003 Skills Strategy includes a safeguard for learning for personal development within ACL, with specific mention of 'pensioners'. A case study of a community IT service looked at a different sort of learning opportunity for older adults in a rural area. There are, of course, many other funded providers whose work is significant for older adult learners, such as the WEA. Colleges have older learners in their mainstream courses, and deliver ACL to older adults in two of the case-study areas, where the services subcontract. There is the University of the Third Age, and many voluntary and community organisations whose work may be unsung. But the case studies provided a test of how far policy intentions interlock in practice with the use of public funding. For practical purposes 'older adults' refers to people from around the age of 55 – that is, people of or coming close to retirement age, and therefore traditionally (but no longer) thought to be nearing or at the end of economic activity.

The case studies

Manchester is an ethnically diverse city, with a population of 392,818. It has gone through dramatic renewal but has 13 wards high on the index of deprivation. People aged 60–69 form 7.5 per cent of the population, and over-70s another 9.7 per cent. Manchester Adult Education Service (MAES) provides both accredited and non-accredited programmes; the majority are directly delivered but it also contracts with 14 agencies to reach particular groups. In 2003/4 it had about 15,300 learners on LSC-funded programmes. Of these, 19.3 per cent were over 60. There were 2.5 times as many women as men learners aged 60-plus.

Warrington has a population of 191,080, and a mixture of deprived 'inner' wards and more prosperous suburban wards, with a comparatively smaller ethnic minority population. People aged 60-69 form 9.3 per cent of the population and over-70s another 10 per cent. Warrington Borough Council (WBC) secures primarily non-accredited programmes, the vast majority by contracting with the large further education college. In 2003/4 it had about 5,400 learners on LSC-funded programmes. Of these 37.9 per cent were over 60, with women in the majority. Warrington also provides a fund for widening participation from its own resources, which is used to grant-aid development work with voluntary and community organisations.

Cheshire is a mixture of prosperous commuter belts, market towns, rural hinterland, and some manufacturing areas, and has a population of 673,788. Some wards in the 'old' manufacturing areas are high on the deprivation index and there are 'pockets' of rural poverty. The Cheshire–Warrington economy is growing fast.

Just over 10 per cent of the population are aged 60–69 and 12 per cent over 70. Cheshire Lifelong Learning Service (CLLS) provides mainly non-accredited programmes. Over 75 per cent of provision is secured through contracts with colleges, but a growing proportion through partnerships with schools and voluntary and community organisations, and a small proportion delivered directly. In 2003/4 it had about 18,000 learners on LSC funded programmes. Of these, 30.8 per cent were over 60, with three times as many women as men.

Switch on Shropshire (SoS) is a project to increase access to broadband in remote rural areas of Shropshire. The county has a population of 283,173; 10.7 per cent of the population are aged 60–69 and 13.1 per cent over 70. SoS began in 2003 and is funded by the Shropshire Rural Regeneration Zone and ERDF (Objective 2). It is managed by the County Council through the Rural Community Council. Its target is to set up 35 'broadplaces' by 2006: these are IT access points planned and managed by the local community. There is already a high proportion of older adult users. Activities include informal learning and the beginnings of some more organised learning provided by local colleges or the adult education service.

> *The Mayfair Centre, Church Stretton* is in the town centre. It has a wide range of services, including the broadplace; 90 per cent of centre users are over 55, with a good proportion over 70. It has about 200 volunteers, most retired. Over 50 people use the broadplace weekly and in 2003/4 86 followed LEA-funded IT courses, almost all over 60.

The higher proportion of older adults in the counties reflects their popularity as retirement areas (and in Shropshire possibly some depopulation from younger age groups). The 2001 census figures show that the proportion is growing in all the case-study areas.

Participation

NIACE's most recent survey shows a fall in the participation rates for those aged 65 or over, within the context of an overall fall in the numbers of current and recent learners (Aldridge & Tuckett, 2004). Fourteen per cent of those aged 65–74 are current or recent learners, compared to 19 per cent in 1996 and 20 per cent in 2002; for those aged 75-plus the figure is 10 per cent (15 per cent in 1996 and 10 per cent in 2002). However, in the 55–64 group 30 per cent are current or recent learners (25 per cent in 1996, 30 per cent in 2002).

The 2003 *Pathways in Adult Learning Survey* (PALS) reports that 16 per cent of over 60s were found to be 'long-term learners' (that is, they had done some learning in the three years up to the *National Adult Learning Survey* 2001 and between then and PALS) compared to 44 per cent of those aged 40–59 (Snape, 2004). They were also less likely to become 'new learners' (to have learnt between 2001 and 2003, but not earlier – 31 per cent compared to 40 per cent), and far more likely to be 'non-learners' (to have done no learning in the whole period – 65 per cent compared to 21 per cent). If they did become new learners it was very unlikely to be for vocational purposes (here, present or future employment or voluntary work).

In the case-study services, the proportion of learners aged 60-plus was greater than the proportion in the LEA's population as a whole – markedly so in Cheshire. Women aged 60-plus were far more likely to be learners than older men, as is typical in many ACL settings. In Cheshire and Warrington, older adult learners were much more likely to come from the more affluent wards, whereas in Manchester participation broadly corresponded to the age profile of wards. In all three areas, some centres or classes were dominated by 60-plus learners. On the other hand, all the services could identify particular groups which were under-represented in terms of ethnicity, gender, social class or disability, and when generally under-represented groups were engaged it was often through project or partnership activities rather than in the mainstream programme. Fourth-age adults are generally under-represented, in spite of the growing population. It is not possible to say how Switch on Shropshire contributes in percentage terms, because the project is at an early stage (and there would be some overlap with providers' figures): it is already showing that older adults can be included in tackling the difficult issue of rural participation.

These figures show how important ACL services are for older adults. But they also caution against seeing 'older adults' as a single group. Apart from the difference between the third and Fourth Age, and differences within the pre-retirement / Third Age group, participation differs according to length of initial education, qualifications gained, socio-economic status, health / disability and – one might add – habit. Ethnicity is an important factor: starting from a lower overall level of participation, Pakistani and, most of all, Bangladeshi adults show a sharp decline in participation after 55.

So the case studies suggest that there is not necessarily a 'problem' about participation in learning by all older adults, at present. If the downward trend shown in NIACE surveys continues, we would need to understand whether it is a supply- or demand-side issue. Changes of policy for funding and fees may modify comparatively high local levels of participation in ACL. But there is certainly a problem about continuing patterns of non-participation and exclusion and about the range of opportunities for particular groups or to meet particular needs.

The benefits of learning

The 'wider benefits' of learning are now well understood: that participation benefits older adults in terms of physical, mental and emotional health, keeps them active longer and enables them to be active in family, social and community life. But as learning gain is currently seen as a crucial indicator of quality, it is useful to note that the 'wider' benefits go hand in hand with those related directly to learning.

> Many of the older learners in Visual Arts spoke with enthusiasm about the way their learning had not only helped them develop new skills and interests, but had also improved the quality of their lives ... an important and valued benefit to their social lives, helping them to sustain their physical and mental agility.
>
> (Warrington LEA Adult Learning Inspectorate Report, 2003)

The latest LSC Satisfaction Survey shows that high proportions of both the 55–64 and 65-plus age groups using ACL providers felt that they had gained greater enthusiasm for their subject, were more creative and prepared to try new things, and were more confident in their ability to learn, as well as benefiting in health and their sense of wellbeing (LSC, 2004). Thirty-one per cent of 55–64s, and a surprising 19 per cent of those aged 65-plus, have learned new skills for their job (the survey covered all work of ACL providers, and therefore included accredited courses). The PALS survey data suggest that these may be the 'long-term learners' of the age-group rather than those with low skill levels. If so, this is yet another reflection of how the learning divide continues.

The University of the Third Age (U3A), which offers many social and informal learning activities found that the most frequent reason for joining was 'social contact' (29 per cent) while 18 per cent wanted to follow an interest, 14 per cent to learn and gain knowledge, 12 per cent to learn new skills, 10 per cent to meet people with similar interests, and 10 per cent to keep their mind active (U3A).[1] This mix of the social and the educational is typical of local IT learning centres too, and has an important bearing on the ways of learning available to older adults (see below, 'Good practice').

Manchester's consultation with older adults shows how sociability in learning creates social capital as well as individual gain: 'Learning which helps older people reflect on their life and cultural histories strengthens a sense of community belonging ... Many older adults are concerned with the quality and security of their communities and want to plan an active role in community leadership.' (MAES, 2003).

Policies and planning

21st Century Skills refers to learning in later life:

> Others pursue learning for its own sake. They have enrolled ... with no intention of getting qualifications ... There must continue to be a broad range of opportunities for those who get pleasure and personal fulfilment from learning. A civilised society should provide opportunities to enable everyone, including those who have retired, to learn for its own sake. (4.40)

---

1 www.u3a.org.uk

We want to safeguard a wide range of learning opportunities for pensioners. There is good research evidence that older learners can benefit substantially from continuing to learn. For many, it represents an important form of social activity. There are benefits to mental and physical health. It may help them support learning within the family or community, as well as pursuing hobbies and leisure interests. While strengthening support for skills, training and qualifications which will support our wider economic goals, we want at the same time to ensure the continued availability of learning opportunities for pensioners which will give so much benefit and pleasure. At present there is wide variation between different areas in the range of learning available, and the fees that are charged for it. It is right that local discretion should remain. But we expect pensioners to benefit substantially from the arrangements for safeguarding funding for leisure learning, and that in all areas learning for pensioners would be one of the priorities through the new planning and funding arrangements. (4.48)

(DfES 2003a)

This commitment has been widely welcomed – but has its limitations for older adults. It gives learning for 'pensioners' a persuasive rationale, but by inference contrasts it with learning to support economic goals. The use of 'pensioners' seems to imply that learning to earn is not an interest or issue. And these are statements about the third, not the Fourth Age: questions of the relative roles of the social and health services are not raised.

The case studies show that, translated to local level, the intentions of the White Paper may play out differently. *21st Century Skills* says that:

Each LSC will decide with its local partners ... the priorities for spending those funds [ie the safeguarded funds] in order to maximise the civic, social and cultural gain for the area. ... The LSC will specifically consider with its partners what first step and return to learn opportunities are available ... (4.42)

The objectives for ACL in the plans of the two local LSCs covering the case-study ACL services are:

- to review how 'other FE' and ACL funding is used to make sure delivery is relevant and contributes to targets ... Increase the emphasis on progression from ACL as first step learning (LSC Greater Manchester, 2003);
- to increase adult participation and achievement ... ACL as first rung provision (LSC Cheshire and Warrington, 2004).

Skills for Life and 'first-rung' provision in ACL are given prominence by the framework within which the local LSCs construct their plans, and the national targets themselves, and the plans do not yet reflect the scope of paragraph 4.48 of the White Paper (even though the latter is about what exists rather than creating something new).[2] This may in turn lead to a perception amongst their staff that other areas of ACL are not important. Further, the requirement to include 'employer engagement' objectives within services' Three Year Business Plans, and the importance attached to working with employers in local LSCs' plans, may suggest that development work should focus on this area, particularly linked to *Skills for Life* objectives. This was the priority accepted by one service. None the less, the services' own plans do refer to older adults.

- Manchester's plan includes the principle that 'older adults should be able to access a wide range of opportunities and services that are culturally sensitive', with objectives for working with voluntary and community groups, widening participation, information, and consultation.
- Warrington's aim is to 'maintain wellbeing and quality of life by engaging older citizens as meaningful learners'.
- Cheshire specifies 'older and disadvantaged adults within the third and Fourth Ages' as a target group for widening participation.

LSC priorities seem not yet to have led to cuts in provision affecting older adults in the case-study areas, with the possible exception of Shropshire. But services feel a degree of pressure and precariousness in relation to non-qualification bearing programmes and provision for older adults within these. They are uncertain about how the funding safeguard will work out (or might be pre-empted), and in consequence find it difficult to engage in meaningful planning for the mid-term or to manage change in relation to provision for older adults. Priorities and attitudes may properly vary between LSCs, but this adds to the difficulty for services of interpreting and responding to national priorities. For example, one service is pressed by its LSC to reduce the number of partners with which it subcontracts because of national policy to limit the proportion of 'franchised' provision to 5 per cent of an institution's work. But another is encouraged to increase the number of partnerships with the voluntary and community sector, as the franchising policy is understood not to apply ACL services which have traditionally subcontracted. Both cases impact on services' ability to reach older adults.

At present, therefore, there is a discontinuity between services' recognition in their plans of the needs of older adults and the priorities of LSC planning. The practical result is that improvements for older adults may well be included in other work but not necessarily tackled in their own right. There is a tension for ACL services between the strong policy aims for older adults being developed by local authorities like Warrington and Manchester and the extent to which their ability to respond may be limited by the very different learning and skills agenda. The issue of fees exemplifies this tension.

---

2   For comparison: the LSC plans do not include reference to the Neighbourhood Learning in Deprived Communities Fund (NLDC), presumably because this is a separate earmarked source. This underlines the extent to which the plans do not now seem to deal with broader issues of regeneration and well-being, which would include the needs of older adults In addition, the Equality and Diversity Impact Measures (EDIMS) used by the LSCs do not include participation by older adults

Rationales and provision

It is not easy to unpick the rationales for what is offered to older adults, particularly when provision has developed historically. In different contexts the rationales at work might be:

- Entitlement: that we should all be able to access learning for personal development and wellbeing, and older adults might have a particularly strong claim to this.
- The 'wider benefits' argument described above.
- Widening participation: that under-represented groups of older adults have a particular claim because of the cumulative exclusion they have experienced.
- Changing patterns of the Third Age: not only do new learning interests emerge as we grow older, but the lengthened period of the active Third Age makes new demands on individuals and society. These might be to do with transition, addressed for example by pre-retirement courses. Or they might be about learning related to work.
- The 'medical model': that ageing or old age mean a series of innate and progressive characteristics; educational interventions help to manage or alleviate these. (By contrast, the 'social model' would distinguish the ways in which society defines ageing and is de facto organised to exclude older adults.)

21st Century Skills uses a combination of the 'entitlement' and 'wider benefits' rationales. Locally, the 'wider benefits' and 'widening participation' rationales are more invoked.

In practice, historic patterns dominate local provision, and this can be interpreted both positively and negatively. Mainly in middle-class areas there is a high proportion of older adult users, particularly in the daytime. In some centres and subjects such as art they predominate and some courses are over-subscribed. In this sense provision might be said to be demand-led and in effect some classes are 'for' older adults. Managers might argue that older adults maintain the viability of the programme, if not of individual classes then of the curriculum range overall, and that this is proper provision for ACL services to make as it plainly matches the learning interests of many older adults. The negative view is that this approach effectively imposes rationing: it is difficult to change what is offered, because this might detract from meeting targets and because of public resistance, and as a result funds are not available for innovatory work to reach older adults who are not participating.

The 'club' question is a further challenge. Providers have long recognised the problem of classes being dominated by repeat enrolments by older adults, so that literally or metaphorically there is no room for newcomers. Professionals may argue over whether it is possible to continue to identify learning gains over long periods of class membership, but inspectors tend to be sceptical. A solution is to see membership of a formal class as finite, and to plan for groups to move on to more self-directed learning. This would both tackle the need to demonstrate progress towards learning outcomes, and free up resources for new participants. Manchester is working on these lines and has designated some courses as '50-plus'. However, the change can meet with resistance: a class may dislike the new style, and may also feel that it is being discriminated against by being offered what members see as a reduced service. In such cases, learners clearly believe in the 'entitlement' model. (Attitudes about entitlement are discussed further under 'Fees' below.)

Generally and unsurprisingly the most popular curriculum areas amongst older learners using the case-study services are ICT, visual and performing arts, hospitality, sports, leisure and travel. Language learning is also popular.

The largest-scale examples of 'widening participation' for older adults are opening up access to ICT and the internet in 'silver surfers' courses and the like. Established services do this not only in adult centres but through partnerships with libraries or taking laptops into older people's centres or housing. Switch on Shropshire is based on the principle of bringing access to broadband in a rural area to the level enjoyed in urban areas, and widening participation goes hand in hand with a distinctive approach characterised by community leadership and a continuum of informal and formal learning.

The case-studies have other valuable examples of widening participation for particular groups of older adults, such as:

● working through groups in particular ethnic communities to meet community needs in a culturally appropriate way – for example, a Chinese women's association (Manchester), Hindu over-50s club and Islamic Centre (Warrington);
● tasters and programmes in day centres and residential accommodation (Cheshire, Manchester);
● funding to carers' organisations for courses to raise confidence and interests (Warrington);
● volunteer training for the Commonwealth Games (Manchester).

All these examples are not about access to existing provision but about doing it differently. Funding is the great barrier, because of the difficulty of diverting from existing provision, but also because the current funding regime is not perceived to enable relatively small-scale development work. One very successful example of negotiating a programme with learners in day and residential centres in part of Cheshire, which is now using mainstream funding, has not been taken up by other providers, and it is presumed that this is because of the development phase costs.

The 'medical model' is not overtly used by any of the services studied but in practice may influence some provision, such as exercise classes. One interviewee thought that it was more pervasive amongst staff than one might expect: this would affect how the curriculum was designed and tutors' expectations of learners. One might also surmise that issues about the medical model would need to be resolved in joint work with health or social services.

It's useful to compare the principles and activities of U3A. U3A embodies both 'entitlement' and 'wider benefits' ideas, but its key principle is that of self-help and activities are therefore self-financing. It might be said to reflect the 'changing patterns' rationale: it depends on a social rather than medical model of ageing, and reflects the needs of the long and active Third Age. Membership at July 2004 was 141,514, with 540 autonomous groups nationally (there were twenty groups across the three ACL service areas). An earlier survey reported that 21 per cent were group leaders; 25 per cent belonged to two groups, and 11 per cent to five or more. The profile of U3A members is overwhelmingly middle class: a very high proportion had been in professional, clerical, supervisory, administrative or managerial occupations; the vast majority had other income than the state pension and lived in their own home. Their learning interests and motives do not seem to differ from those attending mainstream adult education, and indeed a member survey showed that in the last three years 32 per cent had joined an adult education course. U3A has found that the most frequent method used by groups is 'informal study/discussion with input from all group members', followed by 'structured study/discussion, steered by one but with input from all'. U3A's success suggests that subject areas may not matter as much as organisational, social and learning styles, and provides a valuable gloss on the acceptability of self-directed learning.

Learning and work

As already observed, *21st Century Skills* seems to assume that older adults, at least 'pensioners', do not need training which relates to paid work – although over-50s may be tacitly included in the training needs of the workforce. In the north-west, the Framework for Regional Employment and Skills Action (FRESA) anticipates 'changing occupational and employment patterns to meet the needs of an older population and a potential labour market shortage' (NWDA, 2004). Local LSC planning documents refer to the ageing population, the need to 're-skill' older workers to fill skills gaps, and the level of economic inactivity amongst over-50s. They do not include any specific measures for older adults in their plans, though they might well be served by other local actions, just as by local initiatives in deprived communities. At present, training objectives for older adults appear only through Job Centre Plus and the New Deal for 50+ and therefore impact on only a relatively small part of the labour force. Possibly where labour shortages are already leading employers to encourage older workers to stay on, some training may be organised accordingly. But low comparative rates of training for the older workforce at present, particularly women workers, suggest that we cannot assume that their needs will be taken care of.

The Skills Strategy and local planning do not, then, acknowledge the challenge set by the 2003 pensions green paper (TAEN, 2003). How do we enable adults not just to resume or hang on to paid work until state retirement age, but to continue work in a positive way from the late 50s into the 70s? The DfES *Challenging Age* research project found evidence of 'unmet desire that significant numbers of under-performing older people have to work, learn and develop their careers' (DfES, 2004).

In the case-study areas, work-related learning for older adults seems to fall into a gap between providers. It is not considered to be within the remit of ACL services, although one service was well aware of the need, and FE colleges do not appear to have specific priorities or provision. However, older adults may well be using both ACL and FE courses for work-related purposes. This is not easily visible but the LSC Learner Satisfaction Survey suggests that it is significant in ACL, and one of the case-study services thought that older adults were using their provision to change direction.

If we think in terms of a renewal of working life in the Third Age, learning for work will need to be individually negotiated, with access to small units which build on experience, complement existing qualifications, and fill gaps, and with greater acceptance that intermittent learning is legitimate. Older learners may use ACL because it responds to these needs, with locally accessible shorter courses, not necessarily leading to full-scale vocational qualifications. Guidance and support services will need to be extended and redesigned to support this process, as *Challenging Age* points out.

We need to agree that present models of achievement based on full qualifications, and the accompanying targets may be appropriate to young people and younger adults but are not to older adults. The Skills Strategy commitments to unitised qualifications, better assessment of prior learning and a credit framework will all help older learners, particularly if they are accompanied by fee concessions comparable to those for full-time courses. But much higher visibility for work-related learning for older adults will be needed to support the Department for Work and Pensions' policy objective of flexibility in the length and pattern of working life. At present, ACL services (and FE colleges) are probably making a larger contribution than is realised, but for people who can find their own way through the system. This is an area in which ACL services could extend the employer-related objectives of their business plans and where participation targets might help to raise awareness and visibility.

A Cheshire Case Study: Pam's Story

Pam, aged 55, took up a craft course 'Making Books' through her local LEA ACL provision because she had always enjoyed art at school and now as she was not employed she had the time to indulge the interest. She enjoyed the course and progressed rapidly, as do many adult learners who bring to their learning considerable skills acquired during a lifetime of achievement in a wide range of activity. She quickly followed with a 'Book Binding' course and then became a part-time ACL tutor herself. The money from the part-time teaching was put to good use to support herself through an Art Foundation year at the local FE College and she subsequently gained a place on a degree course in Architecture. Following a very successful 1st year Pam had to take a year off as she was the sole carer for her mother. Sadly Pam's mother died during that time. However, Pam is now back on her degree course, and accepting commissions for book binding, interior design and building renovation, all of which help to fund her learning. She is also planning to rejoin an ACL class which, as she says herself, provides continuing learning not only through the curriculum and the opportunity to refine and extend specialist skills, but also through the artistic stimulation and collective knowledge provided by the other adult learners.
Complete changes of career and direction which start from what could be classed as 'leisure learning', and as such not a high priority for government funding, are not uncommon in ACL. It also often provides the route back into a full and active role after the kind of challenging periods that we all face at some time in our lives.

Other unmet needs

How far are the learning interests and needs of older adults being met? In some middle-class areas where there are well-established adult programmes from a range of providers, with high recruitment and satisfaction levels, the answer must be 'Yes, to a large extent'. As the size of the 60-plus population increases there may be unmet demand in such areas in the future (some classes are reported to have waiting lists already). In some rural areas the position may be improving because of the extension of access to IT.

But other groups certainly have unmet needs. Barriers need to be removed, accessibility needs to be improved, and the curriculum negotiated anew. The case studies, drawing on local consultation as well as demographic information, suggest that the following areas need attention:

- Literacy and numeracy: performance levels are much lower amongst people over 55 (DfES 2003b). The current focus on the workforce tends to exclude older adults, who in any case need to be able to access learning on their own terms with appropriately designed curricula. Creating 'embedded' literacy and numeracy learning may be the most valuable approach. Financial literacy learning might also be extended.
- Access to ESOL for some older members of black and minority ethnic communities – but also culturally appropriate learning for BME communities which goes beyond ESOL.

- Access to learning for older adults in deprived communities.
- Provision for adults in the Fourth Age using day centres and residential homes to improve the quality of their lives, and a recognition of short-term learning needs.
- Learning for people with learning difficulties as they age.
- Better opportunities for older adults with mental illness, late onset illness or impairment, chronic illness or disability, and more health-related courses generally. Professionals agree that disability is under-reported at enrolment, perhaps because learners only report if they think it is relevant or want extra help.
- More opportunities to learn through ICT and not only to learn basic ICT skills: ICT learning centres show the scope for this.
- Inclusion of older relatives in Family Learning: this may happen in practice if an older relative has caring responsibilities, but Family Learning programmes (and targets) need to recognise the importance of the role of grandparents and other older relatives and the resource they offer.
- Improving the accessibility of information, advice and guidance to older adults.

A personal observation is that in the programmes of the case studies there is comparatively little about learning linked to transition, other than pre-retirement courses, and that it is difficult to tell how much learning for older adults creates capacity to counter isolation and anomie and to participate in civil society. It seems likely that learning organised in partnership with community groups will do so, but otherwise it is difficult to link such gains to individual activities.

Such a long list of unmet needs suggests that we do need to think about the curriculum for older adults. Typically, services develop the curriculum either through demand-led mainstream programmes or through negotiation with particular groups. Both approaches work within their own terms but they may get in the way of an overview and rethinking priorities.

Partnerships

The case studies emphasise how important partnership working is to reaching older adults – with voluntary organisations and community groups; social and health services; other local authority services. For example, all three services work with Age Concern. Cheshire reaches many older women in rural areas by funding the Cheshire Federation of Women's Institutes. Manchester works with libraries on community and cultural history projects, and Warrington on IT-based learning. Resources can be pooled in inter-departmental work: through shared investment in IT kit, or by library or social services staff working alongside tutors. But services face three major challenges to making partnerships work.

- Bureaucracy and assessment: many voluntary and community groups find LSC recording and reporting requirements, and those of the inspection framework, too burdensome. This puts relationships under pressure. Social services staff, and indeed tutors, often consider requirements about assessment and recording outcomes particularly burdensome or unsuitable for day centre or residential service users. Library staff (and again, tutors) may think assessment requirements inappropriate to the informality and fluidity of the learning.

- Training and commitment: staff in other departments and agencies need training to understand the purposes of learning and how they can motivate and support service users. Managers need to be persuaded that learning should be an ongoing commitment.

- Who pays? In the case of day or residential services, costs may be high because of numbers and the need to maintain care standards. Should learning be seen as part of the care plan? Does learning substitute for other care services? If so, should social services be paying for the learning (effectively contracting with the education provider for provision) or should there be joint funding, with each partner contributing according to their remit? In the case of libraries (or other cultural institutions) informal learning is a part of their role: but does this extend to more than casual help and advice?

Switch on Shropshire's broadplaces rely on partnerships with education providers for more organised learning and their experience gives us a consumer view. Here, the challenge has been to persuade providers that they should work through the broadplaces at all. While one college has seen the potential, another has rejected it (in Shropshire, the LEA subcontracts with colleges). The ACL service was at the time of writing considering withdrawing funding from one broadplace, after a successful year, because of the service's failure at reinspection and subsequent referral to the local LSC for emergency action. It is a familiar complaint from voluntary and community organisations that education providers do not commit to long-term relationships or understand the value which their partners offer. In the case-study LEAs this was not the case, rather that they themselves experienced pressures which made long-term commitment difficult. Shropshire's experience supports the argument that without explicit policy commitments and expectations of good practice, the potential of reaching older adults through community-based work will be missed.

Good practice

The case studies and other examples reveal some particular characteristics of good practice in working with older adults which bear on policy and funding.

Mixing social activities, informal and more formal learning

As the surveys show, social contact is one of the most important motives and benefits for older learners. The lesson of many community IT learning centres that a seamless approach works, in which learning is a natural part of what is happening in a friendly environment. More formal learning flows naturally out of informal learning and back into the community – for example, in one Shropshire broadplace, older adults organised a course in web design to create a website for a local club. The programme for the Hindu over-50s club in Warrington is another example: IT, crafts, yoga, board games, flower arranging. The U3A mixes study with leisure activities and outings.

Sociability is also about learning styles

In Suffolk, a group of mainly older learners in a computer club has sustained its learning over four years by setting its own agenda and format for its sessions.[3] An 80-year-old member of the group wrote:

> We cater for both young and older ladies and gentlemen who wish to keep up with modern technology, but would prefer to do so in a sociable way. And without appearing foolish. We have accomplished this in a relaxed and happy atmosphere with a great deal of encouragement from our tutor.

Similar points about atmosphere can be found in accounts of other IT centres and in inspection reports of ACL services.

Negotiation and self-directed learning

U3A members have written on-line learning courses. Switch on Shropshire is looking at Webquest tools for self-directed learning. The Cheshire example of a negotiated programme in day and residential settings has already been mentioned. U3A groups not only negotiate their programmes of activities but in some activities negotiate together the content of each session.

Challenges

Learning for personal fulfilment means more than conventional 'learning for leisure'. Hillcroft College offers a short return to learn course for women over 55 who have few formal qualifications.[4] The Commonwealth Games volunteer training programme involved many older adults and some chose to join in further volunteering and training after the Games.

Consultation

Manchester has a systematic programme of consultation with learners. There is an annual 'learners' voices' conference and consultations with elders from minority ethnic communities and with users of day and residential services. The results have

---

3   NIACE Older & Bolder email group communication.
4   www.hillcroft.ac.uk

influenced the service's Three-Year Business Plan. In Warrington, the service supports a voluntary sector learning network led by the Council for Voluntary Service and this is a channel for consultation and identifying need.

Ownership

The partnership model of Switch on Shropshire is a functioning network of groups and interests in each community, facilitated in the first instance by the project but then self-sustaining. Each broadplace has a management committee, with representatives of older adults working alongside others and this promotes intergenerational activities and breaks down isolation. U3A groups are entirely self-managing.

The implications are:

- We should avoid stereotyping or patronising assumptions about the interests of older people or their capacity to decide and organise for themselves. The mainstream curriculum in ACL services seems to suit present users. But although development is limited by funding and planning constraints, there is plenty of evidence that older adults' interests and preferences are as diverse as any other group's.

- U3A's success raises the question of whether its principle of self-management would work in different environments if the problem of affordability could be cracked (U3A groups have to meet all costs themselves). Could the principle be incorporated into ACL service planning? It might be as an extension of the practice of grant-aiding or contracting with voluntary and community organisations. One service has already had some demand from groups of older learners to fund them directly, as an alternative to facing a fee increase by the subcontracted college which might make the group unviable. To promote self-management successfully would require greater funding flexibility and a lightening of bureaucratic requirements.

- Self-directed or negotiated learning, self-management and community ownership mean that the curriculum is more likely to be open-ended and flexible, with evolving rather than pre-set goals. This calls for some flexibility and finesse if systems for recognition and recording of progress and achievement are used (see below). Negotiation also carries development costs, including that of building groups' capacity. And the element of risk must be accepted.

- Sociable learning styles as well as open-ended curricula have a bearing on how external quality standards are designed and used. For example, while it may be reasonable to criticise late arrivals or poor attendance at a vocational class for younger people, it may be quite inappropriate in less formal learning for older adults where the group is prepared to accommodate this and understands why people may come intermittently. Our understanding of what constitutes purposeful learning activity may need to be more about process and less about achievement.

Quality Issues

The Minister of State remarked in 2004:

> … learning for leisure and pleasure is distinct and this should be reflected in the workload of teachers and the experience of learners. I intend making announcements in the autumn which will get rid of pointless exams and assessment in this area of learning. Equally, I intend to get tough on poor quality ACL provision which is being highlighted by too many inspection reports. Insisting pensioners doing aerobics are subject to an assessment is 'bonkers', but ensuring that they receive high quality instruction should be non-negotiable.
>
> (Ivan Lewis MP, Minister for Skills and Vocational Education: John Baillie Memorial Lecture 2004)

So what are the quality issues for older adults?

Recognition and recording of progress and achievement (RARPA)

Current inspection criteria use progress and achievement as a key indicator of quality. 'Success rates' are also used as a performance measure by the LSC. Is RARPA – which may or may not use formal assessment in the sense implied by the minister – a barrier for older learners? Interviewees were in fact positive about RARPA, but for differing reasons. One thought that if the primary mission for ACL is about 'first rung provision' it is essential to develop RARPA or formal accreditation; and some older adults may well value this recognition. Others thought that if RARPA is developed tactfully, without too great formality, and integrated into the natural course of learning, it can enhance the quality of experience – although some subjects such as IT lend themselves more readily than others.

However, there have been protests by learners and tutors about formal recording of learning outcomes.[5] A letter in *Adults Learning* gives a tutor's point of view:

> The needs of older students are being neglected because of the pressures put on LEAs and colleges to 'map' students' progress and produce satisfactory outcomes … Many adults come to classes because they have been attending other projects within the community centre or just come for advice. Most are not interested in certification … I feel that students in classes such as mine can have their progress measured in other ways.
>
> (*Adults Learning*, June 2004)

---

5   A lively correspondence figured on this point in my local paper this summer. Following the adult education service's introduction of work on learning outcomes, both tutors and students protested that this was inappropriate, that their class had worked perfectly well before, and that if they did not follow what they saw as an inappropriate approach they would be deprived of their right to learn.

Lighter-touch approaches to reporting and quality assurance requirements for learning for personal development may resolve the issue for some, but it may remain a barrier for voluntary and community groups and in less formal learning. Interviewees also suggested that there is a particular problem in other provision, such as literacy and numeracy, where the assessment structure may work for younger adults but may be too heavy-handed for older ones.

Quality of teaching

The LSC's learner satisfaction survey reports very high satisfaction rates: overall 94 per cent of learners following non-accredited ACL courses, with 80 per cent 'very' or 'extremely' satisfied and notes that 'older learners' tend to be more satisfied (LSC, 2004). Perhaps these high figures reflect adult learners' reluctance to complain or seem ungrateful. But the survey also finds that over-55s are less likely to experience difficulties on course, suggesting that the present offer matches the interests of the quite well-defined group of existing older adult learners. This is borne out by the frequent comments in ALI reports about how much learners, including older adults, say they value and benefit from their courses. We cannot assume a similar response if participation diversified.

A qualified workforce?

Traditionally, services have drawn strength from recruiting enthusiasts who do not necessarily have formal qualifications. But ACL services must now include qualifications for ACL staff in their business plans. While agreeing with the need for rigorous recruitment procedures and better training programmes, interviewees were concerned about whether the qualification models to be developed by the Lifelong Learning Sector Skills Council would match ACL needs. This is particularly an issue for older adults being recruited as tutors. They are an important reservoir of skills – as their involvement as volunteers in IT centres shows – and this may be the point in their lives at which they are able to share their passions as well as staying economically active. However, lengthy formal accreditation, particularly if there is a requirement for pre-entry qualifications, may be inappropriate or a deterrent.

Unmet training needs

Interviewees were convinced of the need for more professional development for tutors. Current programmes tend to prioritise skills for first-rung provision and work-related training, in line with the LSC priorities. But staff need training to work with older adults, which would focus on understanding the interests of different groups, avoiding inappropriate models, and designing appropriate curricula and learning strategies. One interviewee felt that this was particularly important for basic skills tutors. There should also be joint training with staff from libraries, social and health services who work with older learners.

Funding

The predominant sources of funding for learning for older adults are the LSC and, of course, fees. Case-study services had not found other sources of funding except for some projects. However, in-kind contributions are also essential and can easily be under-estimated. These include tangibles such as the venues provided by voluntary and community groups or other agencies, or staff time in libraries and care agencies; and intangibles such as the work of groups in recruiting and supporting learners or that of volunteers running IT centres. In the Shropshire broadplaces, this must be equivalent to more than one full-time employee in each. (U3A is of course self-financing.) Older adults are in a better position to make in-kind contributions of their own labour than many others and this should inform policy: bluntly, harnessing the efforts of older adults may make provision more affordable. But in turn, groups are likely to resent funding strings which seem an imposition because they do not reflect the group's own contribution (or ethos) and add an additional burden.

The constraints in using LSC funds for grant-aid style funding to partners in the voluntary and community sector are one barrier to developing opportunities for older adults and thus benefiting from contributions in kind.

Warrington provides a comparatively small but very useful fund from its own resources for widening participation projects, which can be used much more flexibly than LSC funding. Once established, translating these and other projects into a form for which LSC funding could be used might be difficult.

Apart from the question of the links between funding and learning outcomes, the biggest constraint perceived in LSC funding was financing development work which did not immediately produce learner numbers. This was contrasted with the spur to development given by the Standards Fund for ACL between 1999 and 2003. Services had not used the LSC Local Intervention and Development Fund for work with older adults, presumably because of its terms of reference, and perhaps also because individual projects would actually be fairly small-scale. By contrast, services liked the flexibility of how the Neighbourhood Learning in Deprived Communities funding worked, and older learners in the target wards have benefited from it, for example in access to ICT learning.

Fees

In the current year, the standard hourly fee in the case-study services for non-qualification bearing courses varied from £1.95 to £2-50. So a typical term's course of 20 hours might cost up to £50, more if one includes costs of materials and transport, or a local premium. It is difficult to tell if this is affordable for older adults because of concessions for those aged 60-plus. One service sets the concessionary rate at 40 per cent of full fee. In another, all the subcontracting colleges set it at 50 per cent. The third had a similar concession until 2004/5, when a subcontracting college chose to withdraw it, to local anger.[6]

NIACE's most recent *Fees Survey* shows a confusing range of practice for non-qualification bearing courses – 'former non-schedule 2 provision' (Fincham, 2004). Forty-five per cent of LEAs and 33 per cent of colleges offered concessionary fees to those over 60, a further 12 per cent of LEAs and 4 per cent of colleges to over-60s not in employment, and a further 6 per cent of LEA s and 11 per cent of colleges to over-65s (Fincham, 2004). Three per cent of LEAS and 1 per cent of colleges offered a concession to those over 50. The concession ranged from 100 per cent downwards, with 50 per cent of full fee being the most common. (There were similar patterns for 'former schedule 2 provision'.) The picture is further complicated by the extent to which decisions on concessions are devolved to local providers or centres in the case of authorities contracting out provision.

Should over-60s receive a fee concession as of right? As a learner, there are reasons why you might think you should, because universal benefits for older adults are common although not consistent. Everyone reaching 'retirement age' in the sense of entitlement to state pension:

- can access bus, tram and rail transport more cheaply at least at some times, through buying a pass or paying a lower fare;
- no longer has to pay prescription charges or for annual eye tests ;
- can enjoy many cultural institutions or sports facilities at a reduced rate;
- can benefit from commercial deals, like reduced insurance charges for those over 55 or 60, or cheap meals or haircuts for pensioners;
- receives basic state pension as of right.

Rationales for the various benefits differ, but the effect for the consumer is to create a sense of 'entitlement', that one can expect certain advantages at pensionable age – because one has contributed to society for so long or just because one should be treated decently as one gets old. My personal observation is that this sense of entitlement is very strong amongst some older adults. Removing or watering down an existing concession offends it.

From a policy and provider point of view, things are more complicated. The principle in *21st Century Skills* is that those outside the priority groups should pay more. It is assumed that a much higher proportion of costs in ACL (and some areas of FE) will be met through fees and this will in practice make it difficult to sustain an automatic concessionary fee for older adults even if the flexibility in principle remains. Nor it is in providers' interests to do so: those making fee concessions outside the 'national categories' are effectively lowering their unit of resource as the price of achieving targets (Perry, 2004). One English county

---

6   In addition, all the services offer concessions to the `national' categories – people on means-tested benefits, all learners on basic skills courses.

commented in the *Fees Survey* that subsidising a 50 per cent concession for older adults meant taking money away from funding local areas of need, and one interviewee also felt that the automatic concession could not be defended.

On the other hand, providers may properly consider that automatic concessions for older adults are right if the local authority has strong political priorities for services to them. Ending concessions would certainly cause anger in the community and political difficulty.

The case studies suggest that, in the opinion of some providers, removing concessions for older adults would impact on numbers and competitiveness. This implies that affordability at current fee levels is an issue. While it is difficult to test this, the profile of older adult participants suggests that this may not be so for existing users (although it might affect multiple enrolments). As a comparison, access to the Internet and some informal training is free in the Shropshire broadplaces, but it is assumed that otherwise users will pay for organised learning; and U3A groups have to be self-sustaining financially. However, affordability may well be an issue for under-represented groups of older adults, even if they do not fall within the 'national' categories for fee remission: in the Fees Survey, one metropolitan borough says of its own provision: 'older learners find the cost prohibitive'. In Manchester, which has a learner support fund, 28.7 per cent of applications in 2003/4 came from over-60s (19.3 per cent of the learner population was 60-plus). Applications were for assistance with fees, course books and materials, and fares. Affordability may become a much greater issue if there is a combination of significant fee increases and ending of automatic concessions.

Whether competitiveness is an issue depends on the locality and how far older adults are prepared to travel. But this is not only about choice between providers: one interviewee thought that some better-off groups of learners might choose to go private, by making individual arrangements with tutors, as has happened before when providers have made unwelcome cuts or restrictions. This affects the range of provision available to all.

Providers, then, may at present be trapped in a historic pattern of fee concessions without a sustainable rationale, and with the prospect of having not only to end these but to impose increases. Some will welcome the lever for change created by the Skills Strategy principles, but the change needs to be managed carefully over time. There would need to be a new approach to fee remission for older adults: not universal but more sensitive than the current 'national' categories of fee remission, and with more thought about what help older adults may need with the additional costs of participation. Planners would need to accept that numbers could well be affected.

And there is a job of persuasion to be done – older learners (and politicians) need to be convinced that they should pay or pay more for learning. This is not a task for local providers working individually and perhaps in a context of competition; it needs a national campaign.

Challenges

Fit for purpose? Only to a limited extent, this paper argues. There is a lack of agility in the system's ability to respond to the interests of older adults, not only in what is funded but in how we understand and value learning, in curriculum innovation, and in constraints on partnership working. Some of this may stem from limitations of perspective on the part of providers or limitations in practitioners' skills. But the fundamental problem is a mismatch between broader political and social realities and aspirations, and how policies for learning and skills have developed.

● Insecurity about the future of 'learning for personal development' and holding on to the idea of a 'funding safeguard' distract from thinking about the real challenges. Not only are there current unmet needs; the level of demand and need by older adults will inevitably *increase*. Do we want to maintain historic patterns of provision for older adults? If so, could a new approach to funding and fees generate enough income to diversify provision? Or should providers be steered to reduce provision for the more affluent older adults and negotiate new programmes to widen participation amongst the less affluent or marginalised – consequently, with a lower proportion of fee income? These issues are glossed over in the Skills Strategy. Whatever can be done, more funding will be needed over time.

● We need to do better at funding and encouraging informal learning and self-managing groups. Funding for learning for personal development should be sufficiently flexible for services to support self-managing groups emerging from more traditional provision, or facilitate new ones, and contribute to voluntary and community groups' costs with a modernised system of grant aid plus professional support. This entails proportionately light touch requirements for accountability and quality assurance. Properly managed, as a part of securing ACL through an LEA or other provider, this strategy would combine good practice and cost-effectiveness, stretching public resources further.

● On the same principle: community-managed IT centres are valuable for older adults but sustainability is an issue. In view of their importance as points of access to learning it would be reasonable for them to receive a modest continuing subvention if they continue to engage older adults (and other priority groups), and ACL services and colleges should be expected to work with them.

● For the under-represented and growing group of older adults using day services, sheltered housing or residential accommodation, we need to think seriously about their learning interests and agree on what the contribution of health and social services to learning should be. Learning contributes to the objectives for which they are responsible. Should it not be included as a matter of course in care plans?

● The models and practice which inform the offer of learning to older adults are varied and inconsistent and organisers and tutors need a better, shared understanding of the interests and needs of different groups of older adults and what constitutes quality in provision for them. A national quality initiative for learning for older adults would support the process of change and innovation, and help providers meet the needs described in this paper.

- Inspection criteria should be developed to reflect the interests of older adults within the funding safeguard areas of learning and take account of less formal learning arrangements.

- *Skills for Life* programmes need to be more accessible in style and structure to older adults, with an acceptance that, as in other areas, the exigencies of formal qualifications may not be welcomed by them.

- What more can be done to encourage experiment and risk, so that new practice in learning for older adults develops? Providers need the flexibility to use their core funding for development work, including transferring good practice promoted by Older & Bolder to their own setting. A national development fund linked to the quality initiative proposed above would increase the pace and reach of change.

- The government's proposal 'Fairness for all: a New Commission for Equality and Human Rights' (May 2004) includes the protection and promotion of the rights of older citizens. It acknowledges the reality of age discrimination, although legislation in response to the European Employment Directive will cover only discrimination in the workplace and access to training. However the Skills Strategy ought to go farther and reflect the need for older adults to stay on in economic activity, with research to establish the nature and levels of need and describe good practice. ACL services and other providers should be encouraged to identify and extend their own contribution to employability and retraining for older adults. And the question of financial support for learners in this group should be re-opened.

- How could or should the framework for planning make work with older adults visible and valued? Targets would not necessarily help unless they can be made sensitive to the complexities of participation – but this might lead to micro-management. Strategic Area Reviews might identify some priorities, although this presupposes that learning for older adults has been seen as an issue. Visibility needs to start with national commitment and the inclusion of older adults in the LSC's strategies for equality and diversity and widening participation. Locally, providers should be asked to include objectives for older adults in their planning and to report on participation and progress. This would feed into preparation for implementing the European Age Diversity Directive in 2006.

Acknowledgements

The help of the following people who generously gave time and information for the case-studies is gratefully acknowledged:

Val Lewis, Community ICT Adviser, Switch on Shropshire;
Alyson Malach, Head of Lifelong Learning, Manchester Adult Education Service;
Hazel Manning, Principal Officer for Lifelong Learning, Cheshire County Council;
Jackie Mantle, IT Coordinator, Mayfair Centre, Switch on Shropshire;
Ros Pilkington, Lifelong Learning Coordinator, Warrington Borough Council.

References

Aldridge, F and Tuckett, A (2004) *Business as Usual …? The NIACE Survey on Adult Participation in Learning.* NIACE.

Aldridge, F and Tuckett, A. (2003) *Light and Shade: A NIACE Briefing on Participation in Adult Learning by Ethnic Minority Adults.* NIACE.

DfES (2003a) *21st Century Skills: Realising our Potential.* The Stationery Office.

DfES (2003b) *The Skills for Life Survey.*

DfES (2004) *Challenging Age: Information, Advice and Guidance for Older Adults.*

Fincham, G (2004) *Fees Survey 2002–2003.* NIACE

LSC (2004) National Learner Satisfaction Survey 2002/3: ACL Providers (Summary Report and Technical Data).

LSC Cheshire and Warrington (2004) Business Plan 2004–5.

LSC Greater Manchester (2003) Annual Plan 2003–4.

MAES (2003) *Valuing Older People.*

NWDA (2004) *The North-West's Framework for Regional Employment and Skills Action: Productivity through Employability.*

Perry, A (2004) *Talking about Fees: Provider Policy and Practice on Course Fees.* LSC.

Snape, D *et al.* (2004) *Pathways in Adult Learning Survey 2003.* DfES.

TAEN (2003) *Response to Developing a National* Skills Strategy *and Delivery Plan: Progress Report.* www.taen.org.uk

4. Older & Bolder: the NIACE campaign

Jim Soulsby, NIACE

In the early 1990s the Carnegie Foundation undertook an inquiry into the Third Age – noting the changing prospects facing adults in Britain who were coming to the end of their major period of employment. The inquiry highlighted the very sharp gap in opportunities and health prospects for affluent and poor adults and called for concerted action to overcome the exclusion experienced by older people in many aspects of life. The inquiry appeared just after the Conservative government had created the Further Education Funding Council and with it a curriculum divide which had the effect of marginalising opportunities for older people looking to enrich the quality of their lives. Tom Schuller, who contributes elsewhere here, led the inquiry's education strand.

When the Carnegie Foundation published its findings, and building on work stretching back to the 1960s, NIACE took a strategic decision to commit itself to a sustained programme of work to highlight the needs of older learners, the haphazard pattern of provision for them, and the wider civic, health and social benefits that accrue from older people's participation in learning.

NIACE'S 'Older & Bolder' programme began its work in 1995, supported by the Carnegie Foundation and the Esmée Fairbairn Trust, with a wide-ranging review of the issues affecting learners over the age of 50.

Initial aims

Older & Bolder worked to:

- Increase the educational opportunities for older people, and reverse the narrowing of the curriculum options and locations for learning which had followed the 1992 Further and Higher Education Act.

- Broaden the base of adult education to encourage different older people to participate. NIACE evidence showed that prior educational experience and the age at which people left initial schooling were great influencers over subsequent participation. It was important in reaching different older people to offer appropriate curriculum content, methods of teaching and learning and locations relevant to their needs, and all at times and costs they could manage. In addition, there was a need to show that a range of agencies outside the formal education sector was providing educational opportunities for older people and that some of these initiatives could provide clues as to how to attract new and different older learners.

- Deepen educational experiences. Society tended to view educational opportunities for older people as peripheral to 'conventional' education and as an area where there were not perceived to be any real societal benefits. NIACE sought to develop arguments to highlight the health benefits of learning, and to encourage other policy developments which could embrace the concept of later-life learning. It also suggested that there were elements of visible 'joined-upness' which showed how some older people might apply their later-life learning in socially important aspects of life: work, volunteering, or intergenerational activity.

- Improve educational opportunity. Quality was always an issue, which extended to seeking ways and means of securing the voices of older people to influence what was provided, where, how and when.

This meant working within the educational systems, with other government departments concerned with older people's issues and the disparate age movements.

The key elements of the Older & Bolder programme were:

1 Building an active network of educators and older people's organisations, as a reference group.

2 Identifying local good practice, undertaking surveys and literature reviews, offering evidence to policy reviews to clarify policy priorities.

3 Publicising and promoting the benefits of older people learning, both to individuals and to society, and disseminating positive images of older people learning.

4 Developing project work – notably a National Lottery Charities Board grant to support initiatives in local areas, involving older people in the planning and shaping of provision.

This work was guided by an advisory group which met three times a year and initially brought together expertise in HE, research, FE, U3A, age movements, and age campaigns (the Carnegie Foundation). The group membership has changed over the years, with newer members representing the DfES, LSC, CRE, and LEAs.

Phase two – embedding

The change of government in 1997 introduced a climate of change – now there was a commitment to promote the benefits of adult learning in all its forms. *The Learning Age*, the DfEE Green Paper published in 1998, spoke of 'learning being good for the soul'.

For Older & Bolder, the production of a business plan in 1998, featuring a list of initiatives we felt needed to be developed, led to the DfEE funding work to collect, collate and distribute the learning testimonies of older learners. This satisfied the first three of our key elements: contacting educators and organisations and identifying good practice; encouraging other older people; reminding providers that older people learnt and benefited like others; and providing 'sound bites' and evocative stories for the ministers of the day to introduce into speeches.

The DfEE also supported work to map, analyse and report on the breadth and depth or otherwise of educational opportunities available for older people in care settings. This was published as the *4th Age Learning Report* by the DfEE in 2000; a free publication badged as part of the government's joined-up agenda 'Building a Better Britain for Older People'.

The publication by NIACE in 1999 of its policy discussion paper *Learning to Grow Older & Bolder* coincided both with the UN Year of Older Persons and the Better Government for Older People (BGOP) programme becoming live through its 28 pilot projects across the United Kingdom. The report was launched at a national BGOP conference focused on later-life learning and funded by the DfEE.

Learning to Grow Older & Bolder made 63 detailed proposals, many of which, as the report noted, would benefit adults of all ages. They included measures for the DfEE to address:

- A call 'for increasing participation in education and training by older people, particularly from the poorest socio-economic groups.
- The case for local education authority Lifelong Learning Development Plans to take account of the needs of older people.
- A particular concern that informal and community-based provision be sustained alongside more formal learning.
- The case for the active involvement of older people in the shaping of provision made for them.
- A concern to secure the role of voluntary organisations in engaging older people's participation.
- A call to develop distance learning and the use of new technologies to develop access for older people.
- The identification of the need for further research on how best to meet the learning needs of frail older learners, whether housebound or in other care settings.

- The recognition that learning opportunities needed to be strengthened for older workers

Subsequent sections extended challenges to local authorities, funding bodies, educational institutions, voluntary and community sector providers, employers, trade unions, and broadcasters.

Other government departments were advised to work with the DfEE to:

- Initiate research on the benefits of older people's engagement in learning, and in voluntary work, as a preventative health and social care mechanism, prolonging active living.
- Ensure that surveys and collection of statistics includes older people, extending across the age range to 75-plus, on a standard basis.
- Promote positive images of older people, through publicity and in employment practices.
- Set an example as an employer, by enabling older workers to make a smooth transition to retirement, with access to new learning opportunities.
- Through the work of the Inter-Ministerial Group on Ageing, the Cabinet Office initiative 'Better Government for Older People' and other departmental initiatives ensure that learning provision is an integral part of support services for older people, and is planned adequately at local, national and regional levels.

The launch of *Learning to Grow Older & Bolder* led to ministerial interest, which culminated in the (now) DfES offering long-term support for NIACE's work on Older & Bolder. Working closely both with the DfES, and with other organisations in areas not funded by central government, NIACE created a work programme which featured activities in all four of the key elements of Older & Bolder:

1 **Network development:** The employment of an Information Officer to deal with enquiries, respond to DfES queries, produce a newsletter, write briefing sheets, develop web pages and set up e-mail discussion groups. Also, NIACE collaborated with the DfES on a national conference on learning for the better Government for Older People Programme.
Many of these contacts led to further work in key areas – for instance with Development Agencies, universities, the Pre-Retirement Association, Lifelong Learning Partnerships, financial organisations and companies, and charities.

2 **Identification and dissemination of good practice:** A major focus on 4th age learning work. A DfES-supported report on educational opportunities for older people at home or attending daycare entitled *Days Out, Days In* was produced by NIACE and published in 2002. It was informed by events mounted with the Open University and Help the Aged.

DfES support for these reports led to Department of Health funding, through its Section 64 programme, a project to examine how such work could be embedded, to find effective ways of obtaining local joint ownership, developing appropriate curriculum, sensitising tutors, considering the needs of care staff and managers and securing ongoing funding.

The East Midlands Development Agency funded 'Experience Works' to develop policy, practice and knowledge around older people's employability. NIACE undertook a literature review for the programme, and was subsequently represented on the steering group which later became a StARS priority group. The Community Fund gave support in 2001 to enable Ann Ankers to write a tutors/practitioners pack, to be published by NIACE, on reaching and facilitating older learners.

3 **Promotion of the case for older people learning:** NIACE collected and published positive images of older learners. Among other initiatives was a project highlighting the educational needs of older people from black and minority ethnic communities. Taped testimonies of older learners' experiences produced in 14 different languages entitled *Mind Your Language!* led to projects in Bradford, Camden Town and Southwark working with Punjabi-, Cantonese- and Somali-speaking communities respectively to collect and record more testimonies in those languages to encourage more older people from minority language communities to engage in learning. They also acted as an *aide-memoire* for providers to remind them of the educational needs of people who might not speak or read English.

NIACE organised the 'Celebrating Older Learners Campaign' in 2000–2001 for the DfES. In 2000 this took the form of the Oldest Learner in England competition which led to Fred Moore, then aged 107, receiving this award at DfES HQ in London, to much media interest. In 2001 regional awards were made to organisations best engaged in arts education with older people. Also in 2001, we co-facilitated a seminar for the then Minister for Lifelong Learning, Malcolm Wicks, with providers and learners.

As part of Adult Learners' Week, and building on Age Concern Cymru's similar initiative in Wales, NIACE set up the annual Senior Learner of the Year awards, with support from the DfES and, initially, Saga. The Fred Moore Institutional Award, to reward and highlight good practice across the country, was set up following his death in 2002.

4 **Project development:** The Financial Literacy and Older People (FLOP) programme was set up, building on initial work with LEA provision in Havering, in association with the Basic Skills Agency and Help the Aged, and supported by further funding from Halifax plc. The report of the DfES and Halifax work was published as *Old Money*, and launched at the Financial Services Authority in 2002.

An ongoing 'liaison' group (with government involvement – Treasury, DWP, DfES, Inland Revenue; the world of finance, including the pensions ombudsman service; age movements; advice and guidance agencies), facilitated jointly by FSA and NIACE, meets intermittently to ensure the issues remain on the Government agenda. (The work was referred to in the DWP Pensions Green Paper in 2002 and will be informing the FSA Capability Strategy on retirement.)

Surrey University with the Pre-Retirement Association (PRA) and NIACE launched its Centre for Research into the Older Workforce (CROW) in 2002. NIACE also acted in advisory capacity for the University's Leonardo project on age 50-plus employment.

The Bournemouth, Poole and Dorset Lifelong Learning Partnership was awarded LSC funds to develop two programmes involving older people. One was for employability and the other for older learners in a range of community settings. NIACE advises both these programmes.
The Centre for Sheltered Housing Studies was awarded EQUAL funding in 2001 to develop educational programmes for older people in care settings (sheltered housing) to help them re-engage with the wider community and enhance the employability of themselves and others. As an example, one project in Newport, Wales trained older residents to work with local asylum seekers to help them gain employment.

Phase three – influencing and informing

Since 2002 NIACE's Older & Bolder Programme has become increasingly heavily engaged in influencing and advising government and others, as education and later-life learning have emerged as areas for development as part of a national strategy for older people.

- In 2000, NIACE produced, as part of the United Nations Year of Older People, a mapping tool for older people to record and display the learning opportunities in their locality, complete with guidance as to how to use the information they had gathered to create more and better opportunities, and better co-ordinate and link what already existed.
- During the same year NIACE, working with the Dark Horse Venture, hosted a 'Listening Event' in Liverpool for Geoff Rooker, MP, Minister for Pensions and then government 'Champion for Older People'.
- The NIACE *4th Age Learning Report* was launched at a national event in 2001 when ministers reported back to older people.
- The UN World Assembly on Ageing presented the government with an opportunity to consult with national agencies on how they should respond to its draft strategy. NIACE contributed to this and also attended the World Assembly Research Conference in Valencia in 2002 which preceded the Madrid Assembly. It was in Valencia that the paper *55Alive!* was introduced. This had arisen from an inquiry by the DfEE on learning opportunities for older people in their '2½th age' – i.e. in the years immediately preceding retirement.

- *55Alive!* gave rise to 'Stage Posts' – arguing for more effective joined-up advice and guidance services for older people, linked to education but also building on government drives in health promotion, financial planning and education, active citizenship and positive ageing. This paper has been widely circulated across government. It builds on a life-stages concept and, we believe, its influence can be detected in the newly proposed LINK-AGE strategy.

- In 2002 the National Partnership Group was created by the government to help inform its 'Third Age' work and support the Cabinet Sub-Committee on Ageing. Chaired by the Minister of Pensions, the group comprises most of the major NGOs working with older people as well as older people active in Better Government for Older People (BGOP) through their Older People's Advisory Groups (OPAG). NIACE has been a part of this process from the outset.

- This involvement has led to consultations with the Inland Revenue, the Treasury, the National Audit Office, Department of Work and Pensions and Department of Health around quality-of-life issues (and the place of later-life learning, whether for employment, making sense of finance and taxation or in care settings).

- In December 2002 NIACE was invited to join the Management Board for the Better Government for Older People programme. However, in 2004 the BGOP management structure changed and what role NIACE might have in the future is not yet clear.

- NIACE, working with CROW at the University of Surrey, undertook a mapping exercise for the Department for Work and Pensions into the awareness and actions of all nine Regional Development Agencies (RDAs) with reference to the forthcoming age discrimination regulations affecting employment, education and training.

- The Department of Health hosted a conference in 2004 for NIACE to disseminate its findings from the Carry on Learning programme funded through Section 64. Stephen Ladyman MP, Minister of State for Health, spoke at this event, which brought together the pioneering work undertaken in Bromley and Calderdale.

Working with the DfES

NIACE's work with and for the DfES continued.

The key elements of network-building and the identification and dissemination of good practice were further developed by a second national conference for BGOP held in Sheffield and drawing together a range of agencies to talk with older people about the value of education in their lives.

A small project was started to explore what curriculum changes had been made that reflected the needs of older people in the 21st century and to see what new curriculum areas could be developed. Working with the Pre-Retirement Association, this initially involved:

- a survey of PRA practitioners to determine their awareness of changing employment and retirement patterns and to elicit their response;
- working with older learners engaged in an Age Concern Surrey education project to discuss learning needs; and
- mapping the provision for older learners in the Guildford area.

The next stage of the project – curriculum development and testing – is currently being developed with Surrey LEA.

A further testing of the financial literacy work was undertaken with older people in Exeter and Bournemouth. Part of the exercise was to see how education providers, advice and guidance agencies and the age movement could work with older people and some of their representative organisations to make things happen in any locality.

In 2004 the DfES worked with NIACE to bring together other government departments, other relevant parts of the DfES and the age movement to consider what policy developments the government should be considering.

The LSC and age diversity

The national LSC had produced guidance for local LSCs on equality and diversity issues that were covered by legislation. Age-related advice was not available as there was no legislative framework. However, the forthcoming age discrimination regulations (2006), the National Audit Office report *Welfare to Work*, looking at government policy to assist older people back into gainful employment, and the creation of the national Equality and Diversity Committee have all presented opportunities for LSC work on age-related issues.

A project to develop an 'empowerment' curriculum was begun. This involved mapping the work being undertaken by Help the Aged through its 'Speaking up for our Age' forums; by Age Concern through the forums its federation was developing; and by OPAG and the wider pensioners' movement. Currently, curriculum development is being explored with Coventry Community Education Service; Age Concern Northampton and County Lifetime Education project, working with a local OPAG; and Leicester Adult Education College. It is hoped that the new curriculum areas can be made available to other providers and disseminated through the LSC, thus encouraging funding.

In 2004 NIACE hosted a seminar for the LSC to ascertain from other government departments and the age movement what its role should be in furthering the education and training needs of older people. This was followed by an internal seminar for LSC staff to determine local interests and concerns.

NIACE supports the LSC Equality and Diversity Director in her work with the new Equality and Diversity National Committee. Currently this involves mapping local LSC interests and actions and writing an age diversity guidance paper for LSC staff.

Work in Wales

Although there was no dedicated worker for older learners in Wales until 2000, NIACE was active around the issues. A Carnegie-funded project had been working with older unemployed people in Rhondda Cynon Taff. One of the first Older & Bolder networks was based in Swansea, centred on the FE College. In 2000, NIACE Cymru was awarded Community Funds to develop a mentoring programme with older people, led by Christine Glover, which operated in the north (Bangor) and South (Port Talbot) of the country.

In 2003, NIACE Dysgu Cymru succeeded in a bid to the Esmée Fairbairn Trust for two years' funding for a Project Worker dedicated to Older & Bolder in the principality. Eirwen Malin's start coincided with a lot of activity from the Welsh Assembly in developing older people's policies and in empowering the voluntary sector through its Age Alliance. The mapping tool of 1999 has been revised for Welsh audiences, and work is also developing around the empowerment curriculum.

Developing issues and themes

Following the aims established at the outset, the Older & Bolder programme has attempted to influence the participation of older people in all areas of adult learning by means of newsletters – 18 over the last nine years; briefing sheets – dealing with topics such as older learners with sight impairment, financial literacy, cultural diversity, mentoring, messages for LSCs, and annual statistics; and its annual conferences – in Bristol, Newcastle upon Tyne; London, Reading, Derby, Coventry, Manchester, Leicester and Leeds.

The publication of the NIACE policy paper *Learning to Grow Older & Bolder* in 1999 summarised all the issues then apparent, including funding, inappropriate curriculum, accessibility and location. However, it was decided through the first business plan that there could be some thematic issues worth developing alongside the general aim of improving participation across all sectors, and it is worth recording progress and issues still in need of consideration.

Fourth Age Learning

This work has developed over six years, starting with the two reports for the DfES and reaching the end of the Department of Health-funded project in 2004.

Unresolved issues which have emerged are as follows:

- There is a high turnover of staff in the care sector, which causes difficulties both in their training and in the inculcation of the concept of lifelong learning as an integral part of care.
- Although the National Service Framework for Older People encourages the development of education and leisure opportunities for older people, there is little evidence of real joined-up work to make this happen.
- LSC funding streams limit the opportunities available. There is little evidence of shared funding.
- Very few providers work to ensure that learning gains or aspirations are recorded and feature in care plans, in considering care needs or in care inspections procedures.
- There is little evidence of cross-sector collaboration, either to develop and embed learning opportunities or to ensure collaboration and coherence between the range of agencies and sectors engaged in care (occupational therapists, community artists, chiropodists, reminiscence workers, health visitors, adult educators, care staff, family and friends).
- There are few qualifications specifically for activity organisers in care settings and none for education providers.

Financial literacy and older people

This was another small project which grew to embrace curriculum development, joint working, liaison between advice and guidance agencies and education; a dialogue between education providers, the world of finance, advice and guidance, older people's organisations, older people themselves and government.

Currently the following work is under way:

- A project funded through the Basic Skills Agency has been testing existing curriculum materials with older people from a range of backgrounds, including OPAG, older women's network, U3A, retired trade unionists and older people engaged in local authority adult education provision.
- From these pilots a handbook for basic skills practitioners is being considered, as well as a report for older people's organisations and adult education providers.
- The reports and curriculum developed as part of the FLOP projects are available on the Older & Bolder webpages and are regularly downloaded.
- NIACE and the Financial Services Authority co-host a 'liaison' group comprising The Treasury, DWP, Inland Revenue, DfES, Age Concern, Help the Aged, Pre-Retirement Association, CAB, Basic Skills Agency and Pensions Ombudsman which considers the entire range of cross-government issues. Many of these were raised in the DWP Pensions Green Paper *Simplicity, Security and Choice: Working and Saving for Retirement* published in December 2002, which mentioned NIACE's work on improving the financial literacy skills of older

people. The liaison group has now linked into the FSA working group considering retirement issues in the future.

Cultural diversity

Raising awareness of the needs of older people from black and minority ethnic communities was first raised through the Mind Your Language programme (see p. 67). In addition:

- one of the three NLCB-funded projects led by Anne Ankers to elicit the learning needs of older people was with the African-Caribbean community in Leicester;

- this community, alongside the Chinese community in Oxford, provided focus groups for the FLOP and Halifax work;

- the DoH Section 64-funded project developing learning opportunities in care settings worked with an older Asian ladies' day-care centre in Halifax; and

- Raxa Chauhan, Older & Bolder Project Assistant, is currently working with a learning programme for older Asian women in Salford, Leigh and Wigan, helping with the programme evaluation by Keele University.

Empowerment curriculum

The recent emergence of a range of older people's forums, together with the development of the Older People's Advisory Groups associated with BGOP and the desire of local and national government to better consult with older people about relevant policy, suggested a need to develop curriculum areas to aid older people in these processes. In particular, it was felt that only through the provision of such educational opportunities would more and different older people participate. For some older people, engaging in such learning to satisfy an immediate need may be a stepping-stone to other areas of engagement including learning.

NIACE's work has been funded by the LSC and has attempted:

- As advised by the BGOP Director, to work with an OPAG in Tameside, acting via the older participants to engage local services. This has not proved to be possible for various reasons, including the unwillingness or incapacity of busy older people to engage in yet another 'subject' area and the fact that such groups often rely on the patronage of local authorities and other service organisations for their continued existence – which can make it difficult for older people to feel they really own their group's agenda.

- To work with a community centre in Leicester, collaborating with all adults engaged in the local community developments, but in particular with the older participants. Local sensitivities made the development of this work quite tricky, and it is only now about to start, funded through the local Lifelong Learning Partnership, and led by Leicester Adult Education College.

73

- To work with Age Concern Northampton and County's Lifetime Education programme in association with one of the county's nascent OPAGs.
- To build on the expertise of the Community Education Service in Coventry and its links to a wide range of older people's groups and learning activities in the city.

From all this work a national programme for OPAG is likely to emerge in 2005, as is a replicable model for LSC dissemination.

Curriculum for Later Life

The rise of 'ageing' as an issue in international as well as national social policy suggests a need to examine the current curriculum available to older people. Annual surveys reveal the worsening participation rate of older people in various sectors of lifelong learning. Location, cost and timing are considered to be reasons for this situation. But so is the relevance of what is on offer. The current interest presents an opportunity to examine what we do offer, to explore how potential older learners' needs are determined and addressed, and to consider what new curriculum areas could be developed.

Like the government in its pensions Green Paper, NIACE believes that more could be done to promote relevant later-life learning through a life-stages approach which considers the decision-making required at certain stages of life and how education, information, advice and guidance can assist in making these decisions.

Current work with Surrey LEA and others is developing and testing new curriculum areas with older learners, and exploring how these could be used to attract new learners.

Life-stages: Education, information, advice and guidance – 'Stage Posts'

NIACE has been consistent in its messages to government and others that one way of ensuring social inclusion of older people is by increased recognition of the importance of life-stages. Adult education is full of examples of people who turned to learning at times of crisis in their lives. The testimonies of Adult Learners' Week winners provide such evidence. Adult education is recognised by government and others as a way of improving financial literacy among the adult population. We believe that case studies developed, promoted and publicised can help people identify with successful learners and encourage them to acknowledge their own needs and seek support.

The government has also funded a different range of measures to better inform older people, particularly in areas of health and health promotion. Many of these initiatives are funded to achieve narrow goals and not provide opportunities for other initiatives to build on their successes.

NIACE wishes to build on these various initiatives to provide linkage with other targeted programmes, cross-sector collaboration and information, and relevant educational opportunities. A paper to foster this notion, 'Stage Posts', has been published in *Adults Learning* (October 2004) and promoted through other networks.

Future challenges

Much of NIACE's work through its Older & Bolder programme has been with government departments and older people's organisations, to encourage the idea that education has a role to play in developing and maintaining a good quality of life for older people. But this has been set against a background where older people's engagement in lifelong learning has been decreasing, because of diminishing opportunity and high expense. The current emphasis on skill enhancement has not benefited older people, who have not always been seen as a part of the economic equation. Nor is this emphasis relevant to people beyond state pensionable age who seek adult and community education opportunities for self-fulfilment, social contact or as a tool for wider societal and community involvement.

The education sector itself, although it is home to many people skilled in working with older learners, has not provided an ideal climate to further their needs.

Quality

With the policy climate slowly changing – the DfES and LSC are now looking at education policy and practice with respect to older people – more needs to be done to identify and support education champions of older people, to encourage wider participation and to ensure quality of provision.

Older & Bolder needs to do more with practitioners not only through curriculum development but also in quality measures and in ensuring that the voice of older learners is heard and acted on in the planning and evaluation of provision.

Keep joining up!

The NIACE financial literacy work is a good example of an approach that builds on a potential curriculum need and engages older people to explore what the issues are, identify curriculum requirements, and evaluate existing curriculum and learning-support materials. But the work goes further than this. It attempts to engage all the relevant advice and guidance agencies, older people's organisations and local consultative forums so that emerging concerns and issues can be addressed whether they are educational (developing a skill or understanding information), guidance-related (how welfare, financial advice and other agencies provide appropriate support and relevant information) or local concerns (to be addressed through forums and similar structures).

This principle of joined-up collaborative working lends itself in so many ways to the task of engaging the disengaged, who may find that education can be of value at times of crisis or when in dependency situations. The NIACE work on learning in care settings work has shown this clearly.

The government's wish to develop 'joined-up' services through its Single Assessment Procedure, SAP, and LINK-AGE (the new Third Age service) present a good opportunity to do more. But, at present, education is not visible in these policy frameworks.

Learning fit for purpose

The National Skills Strategy highlighted the conundrum facing policy-makers who are considering the educational needs of older people. The paper referred to the need to secure good-quality education for pensioners but ignored the potential and actual role of older people in the paid and social economy. Moves to encourage older people to stay in work longer, or to be mentors, or volunteers, together with the publicity campaigns advocating active ageing through societal engagement, all suggest to older people a quite prescribed agenda – one which does not seem to offer any form of education for the exercising of choice.

There is a movement to smudge the definition of, if not eliminate from the vocabulary, the term 'retirement'. Some people will wish to leave paid employment before they reach state pensionable age; others will not or cannot because of financial constraints. Some will wish to leave work in 'mid-life' for a while and perhaps return, others may still be wanting paid employment in their 70s and 80s.

The labour market favours older women but not older men. It favours those seeking low-paid, low-status work with unsociable hours, shifts and or on temporary contracts. Some employers are being flexible in how they employ older people. But none appear to be training older people for work (the New Deal 50+ training grant was only available once people obtained work), training people in work, or training people for life after work.

There does seem to be a need to consider how the education system can better connect with older people to help them reach their full potential, whether as paid employees, in self-employment or consultancy or as grandparents, carers, environmentalists, volunteers, mentors, campaigners or community activists.

The Curriculum for Later Life and Empowerment Curriculum work that NIACE is currently undertaking is leading the way in considering curriculum development relevant to older people in 21st-century Britain, recognising the demographic changes under way and the ways government is targeting older people to play a fuller part in society.

Missing people

NIACE data show that those who leave school the earliest are those who least benefit from adult education later in life, even though it is those people who probably have most to gain. Yet it can be quite problematic to ascertain what those needs are. NIACE's work on its National Lottery-funded project indicated that working where people lived and applying a community-development approach seemed to be the most effective way to build up trust and ascertain need. One of the reasons NIACE has worked with older people's organisations is to encourage them to consider how education can help them individually and collectively.

The mapping exercise undertaken in Southwark and Leicester to test the mapping tool in 1999 revealed the range of 'learning' opportunities already in existence that had no connection at all with the formal system. NIACE needs to do more to build the bridges between these programmes and the formal providers to encourage progression, support and facilitation without threatening autonomy. It is likely that future older learners will come to learning from clubs, associations and activities in their own communities.

Demography

The changes in the population structure are well documented. The increase in the numbers and proportion of older people is an issue to be addressed by all sectors of government and society. The so-called 'pensions crisis' points to the need for increased financial literacy. Changing work patterns partially caused by demography but also a consequence of the increased use of technology and the changing base of work in the UK (less manufacturing industry and more service occupations) also indicate a need for real lifelong learning to help in decision-making, adjusting to change and analysing and satisfying skills needs. Changing family structures give rise to more home-based care, with many older people having to care for their grandchildren or their own parents: family learning policy needs to consider these implications.

Many of the drivers for change arise from the assumed level of dependency of an increasing number of 80-year-olds in the future, with concern over the costs of health and care. Lifelong learning is a 'preventative' measure that could be better utilised now to delay the onset of dependency.

However, of equal concern is that there are and will be fewer younger people to provide the skills and wealth for the country, necessitating a greater reliance on older people and a need for them to stay in paid employment for longer (and, as a consequence, enhance their pension).

NIACE's work in this area is still in its infancy, with many issues to be considered. The ageing of the population is an issue which goes across all our work, and we need to ascertain how it presently impacts, and what the future impact will be, on all the constituencies we work with.

Securing the evidence

The work of the Centre for Research on the Wider Benefits of Learning is producing evidence of the benefits of engagement in lifelong learning. However, this work is not yet being acknowledged in education policy, nor in other government departments such as Health. In addition, the centre has not looked at issues that might be relevant to older learners. NIACE advised the pioneering DfEE-funded study by Dench and Regan *Learning in Later Life: Motivation and Impact* (IES Report/DfEE 1999) which highlighted the benefits later-life learning provided. The government is requesting better evidence-based research to support its policies for older people, and NIACE should be working with the relevant agencies to help secure this.

More Stage Posts

The government's LINK-AGE consultation, the expected older people's strategy, and DfES policy considerations all present opportunities to argue for better and more joined-up services for older people to help them to determine their role and quality of life. The 'Stage Posts' concept has much to recommend it – if not as a model then as an indicator of what should be done. The current interest in the idea expressed by Help the Aged, Job Centre Plus and in parts of government should be built upon. Older & Bolder has been working on life-stages models which show how education and IAG are inter-related and should be better co-ordinated. This work and the interest in it needs to be sustained.

Education about ageing

NIACE's work on learning in care settings revealed the lack of knowledge among professionals and others working with older people about ageing and about the role of other agencies and services in helping older people attain a fair quality of life. There is a lack of collaboration and co-ordination between training and professional bodies about how those being trained can build on or complement the work of others. This is essential for older people in care settings who rely on a range of services provided by professional bodies from different bureaucratic sectors. It is even more urgent as the education sector develops an increasing role alongside health, welfare and housing bodies. The 2004 NIACE publication *Older People Learning: Myths and Realities* is an important component of the nascent educational campaign.

LSC

NIACE's current work with the LSC presents an ideal opportunity to provide guidance for local LSCs in how to work with older people. This will build on the briefing sheet published in 2000, and be based on the findings of the two seminars undertaken for the LSC, a mapping exercise and the results of the DfES seminars in 2004.

The EU age-discrimination regulations 2006

The implementation of the regulations will have an impact across all of education and training and on all ages post-18. There is much work to be done in dissemination, particularly once the draft regulations are produced in 2005.

Envoi

In short, nine years on, and despite recurrent government interest, there still remains a great deal to be done. By providing a national focus on the learning needs of older people, for work and for wider civic engagement; by maintaining active co-operation with other age-related networks, and by sustained advocacy, we have helped build a case for the learning needs of older people. Natural justice and demographic change make this an appropriate time to respond to that change.

References

BGOP (Better Government for Older People) (May 2000) *Making a Difference – The Better Government for Older People Programme Evaluation Report*.

Boaz, Annette and Hayden, Carol, with Dunning, Andrew and Shreeve, Martin (2000) 'Building a Better Society for Older People', Report on the Listening Events to the Inter-Ministerial Group on Older People, University of Warwick, Warwick Business School.

Carlton, Sheila and Soulsby, Jim (2002) *Financial Literacy and Older People Curriculum*, NIACE.

Carlton, Sheila, Soulsby, Jim and Whitelegg, Di (2002) *Old Money: Financial Understanding For Older Adult Learners*, NIACE.

Carnegie UK Trust (1969) *The Third Age: The Continuing Challenge*.

Dench, Sally and Regan, Jo (1999) *Learning in Later Life, Motivation and Impact*, Research Report 183, Department for Education and Employment.

DfES (Department for Education and Skills) (1998) *The Learning Age: A Renaissance for a New Britain*, Command Number 3790.

DfES (2000) *Fourth Age Learning Report*.

DfES (2003) *Learning in Later Life* – a joint Department for Education and Skills/Better Government for Older People Conference - 19th March 2003 Conference report.

DWP (Department for Work and Pensions) (2002) *Simplicity, Security and Choice: Working and Saving for Retirement*.

National Audit Office (2004) Report, – *Welfare to Work: Tackling the Barriers to the Employment of Older People*.

Plewis, Ian and Preston, John (2001) *Evaluation The Benefits of Life Long Learning: a Framework*, Centre for Research on the Wider Benefits of Learning.

Schuller T. and Bostyn A.M. (1992) *Learning: Education, Training and Information in the Third Age*. Carnegie Inquiry into the Third Age. Research Paper Number 3. Carnegie UK Trust.

Soulsby Jim (2004) 'Stage Posts', in *Adults Learning* (October 2004), NIACE.

Soulsby, Jim (2000) *Mapping Learning Opportunities For Older People: The Report*: Mapping exercise undertaken during the International Year of Older Persons for the UK Secretariat & DfEE.

Soulsby, Jim (2002) *Days out – Days in*, NIACE and DfES.

Withnall, Alex; McGivney, Veronica and Soulsby, Jim (2004) *Older People Learning: Myths and Realities*, NIACE.

5. Older Learners – a modest proposal

Alan Tuckett, Director of NIACE

Purpose and context

Older people face starkly different circumstances now. Until a generation ago few men lived more than a year or two beyond retirement; and few adults experienced prolonged good health in the Third Age. The dependency ratio was heavily weighted in favour of young people of working age. Retirement was at a fixed age for most, and the gap between work and leisure was clearly marked. As the UK's industrial base changed, larger numbers of adults were displaced from the labour market in their forties and fifties, never to work again. For some this led to a life of leisure, for more to constrained choices and the risk if not the reality of poverty.

A combination of demographic, geographical, industrial, social and medical changes have altered the picture facing people in their fifties and sixties now. Overall, the demand for jobs over the next decade in the UK will exceed the numbers of young labour market entrants, likely volumes of migrant workers, and realistic expectations of increases in labour market participation by women. Already, in some sectors and some regions there is evidence of older people being encouraged to stay in the labour force, or as in the Thames Valley corridor to return to the market after retirement. The forthcoming EU Age Discrimination regulations, and changing Government policy has led to a climate change – where people are encouraged to work for longer.

The rapid increase in life expectancy has yet to be accompanied by increases in the proportion of retirement spent in good health. There is a significant challenge in preserving the physical and mental health of many older people – to prolong active life and minimise the period of morbidity. Large numbers of older people carry the responsibilities of caring for even older or infirm relatives. This work would otherwise risk overwhelming welfare state services.

The growth in the proportion of daily life spent at work by men and women of child bearing age has placed an increased burden on older people in keeping the fabric of civil society intact, through voluntary work and governance in voluntary and statutory bodies. Older people are a significant resource, too, for inter-generational learning, particularly when family structures are changing and becoming more linear, and grandparents are taking on increased responsibility as carers.

The growth of Saga and other age specific consumer services points to the major growth of a Third Age market for cultural activities, for those with the resources and confidence to make use of them.

Taken together, these forces present older people with a range of choices about how best to spend the last third of life. Those choices will of course change over the life stages – as adults move from active to less active roles. However, there is a sharp divide between well-informed educated and confident older people, able to make active choices, and those facing poverty on inadequate pensions, with few skills and less confidence. There is, too, a sharp distinction between work and society in many of the regulations that shape working lives and inhibit the evolution of more flexible patterns of work, personal and community engagement among older people.

Education and training can play a significant role in supporting older adults to make informed choices about what combination of work, personal development and active citizenship works best for them– but only if a more coherent suite of policies can be developed. It should be the purpose of government policy to develop those policies, in the light of available resources.

Key partners

The Skills Strategy and the *Skills for Life* strategy both have the potential of enhancing choice for older people, and the cohort can make contributions to DfES targets in both areas. However, the economic and social case for investment in learning among older people touches on the concerns of a number of Government departments:

Health

The positive health effects of engaging in learning have been clearly mapped in a range of international studies, drawn together by the Wider Benefits of Learning Research Centre. This autumn's health promotion White Paper, and the recent publication of the Mental Health strategy each point to the importance of these issues. The Department of Health recognised the importance of the learning needs of carers by including the social care sector in the remit of the NHSU (now the NHS Institute for Learning, Skills and Innovation). The National Service Framework for Older People as part of its health promotion strategy highlights the need to engage older people in leisure and learning. NIACE's Prescriptions for Learning project draws attention to the health enhancing function of participation in learning – but there is still a challenge to move perceptions about ageing beyond the medical model.

Work and Pensions

The pensions crisis has highlighted the importance of developing pensions arrangements that allow older people to taper their working careers – and the critical importance of financial planning to effective choices in older life. The size of the cohort of people in their forties, fifties and sixties on incapacity benefit, unable because of current benefit rules to choose modest re-engagement with work and learning, highlights the sharp inflexibility in many of our systems. The Department of Work and Pensions is seeking ways of reducing dependency on incapacity benefit in later years – and there is a clear opportunity for inter-departmental co-operation to identify the role education can play to that end. DWP's plans for 'Third Age' services will need an educational component, too.

Trade and Industry

The Department of Trade and Industry shares with the DfES the concern to ensure an appropriately skilled and qualified workforce is available to sustain a healthy and growing economy. The role older people can play in filling labour market shortages and enhancing productivity is inhibited by exactly those issues of poor formal qualifications, and little access to training that the Skills Strategy highlighted for adults with skills below level 2. The DTI concern with the importance of informal learning, and with improving public policy understanding of how to capture experience based learning will be of real importance to successful strategies for older people. Its Foresight programme draws attention to the role Investors in People can have in supporting employers to retain and reskill older workers. DTI will also have responsibilities relating to the implementation of the EU Age Directive, and the learning dimensions of that, which include a public education responsibility to make the effects of the regulations widely understood.

Home Office

The Home Office has a key interest in promoting the skills needed for successful volunteering; like ODPM, DfES and the Cabinet Office they have a concern with active communities and regeneration – where older people can with confidence play key roles; – an interest, too, in active citizenship, and the integration of minority elders lacking English language skills.

ODPM

The Office of the Deputy Prime Minister has a range of interests – in the role of older people in neighbourhood renewal; in population movements and migration; in contesting fuel poverty; like the Dept of Health a concern with carers through its oversight of the work of local govt. Local authorities take responsibility for support for people in a state of dependency. The contribution learning can make to the quality of care is clearly mapped in NIACE's work on Fourth Age adults.

Culture, Media and Sport

The Department of Culture, Media and Sport, through its oversight of broadcasting, can have a major impact on motivation and participation by older people. Its concerns with media literacy will address the sharpness of the digital divide – which excludes many poorer older people from the richness of choice available with the new interactive technologies; its Sports policies share a concern to secure a more active and healthy nation (cf. recent Parliamentary debates about the value of yoga); and in the arts and libraries there are concerns to maximise informed participation among a growing population of older people.

The Treasury

The Treasury has concerns about financial literacy and financial education more widely. The FSA's work currently lacks an explicit focus on older people's information and learning needs – but the concentration of debt, poverty and lack of confidence among poorer older people is a major concern. The finance world considers that poor financial decision making costs the industry millions of pounds each year in dealing with the results of bad decision making. It believes that a better educated public will lessen the need for regulation in some areas. However, both the industry and the sector have a tendency to confuse better information supply with improved financial education.

Education

The Secretary of State might consider building on the success of the inter-departmental Skills Alliance by co-ordinating a similar cross departmental group for taking forward learning strategies for older people.

Whilst the ELLFS data and the LSC's report on participation both point to a recent increase in participation among people over 60, this cohort is markedly less engaged with learning than any other population segment. The learning divide, like the income gap, is starker among older people. The *Skills for Life* strategy has been less successful at reaching and engaging older people with weak literacy, numeracy and language skills than the rest of the population; IAG services are less effective at reaching the older age cohorts than younger people; and older adults get less opportunity to learn at work.

Yet this generation of older people have paid more taxes for education, and derived less benefit from the system than any other. The overwhelming majority learned early that education was not for the likes of them, and left school without formal qualifications. As a result motivation and guidance need to be key elements of a successful strategy.

The DfES should consider what can be done now with at most modest injections of new money, what can be done in alliance with other departments and what might be offered in the future. Reviewing policy now would be timely, since the implementation of the EU age diversity directive in 2006 is likely to impact on all forms of publicly funded education for adults.

Skills for Life

Given the new targets up to 2010, and the current pattern of take-up of literacy, language and numeracy provision, a specific programme focus should be developed to make *Skills for Life* accessible to older people. One dimension of this is enhanced investment in numeracy and financial literacy for those older adults living in, or on the borders of poverty – to avert debt, and to increase choice fore people.

Skills Strategy

For many people over 45 it will be daunting to sign up to a whole level 2 qualification – yet piecemeal over time many will enjoy enhanced working lives through gaining the qualification. Can a 45-plus pilot for fee exemption for adults committing to partial achievement of a Level 2 qualification be considered? Many older people seeking to extend skills and prolong their working lives will have high levels of skill acquired informally. Finding a fit for purpose mechanism to accredit this experience for older adults may help with the target and enhance learners' choices.

Clear guidance needs to be issued to secure the curriculum range for the work protected under para 4.48 of the Skills Strategy. (Cornwall LEA in the late 90s adopted a policy of at least one class in every village) There is a danger otherwise that LSCs locally will make crude decisions that make the guarantee undeliverable. The key challenge is to invest enough to widen participation for older people who have little confidence, and no history of participation, whilst managing the move to higher fees for those people who can afford them. One measure for the LSC remit should be to secure rising levels of participation by older people, until they are not under-represented.

A focus on using 4.48 to promote effective strategies for people recovering from mental health problems will have a direct benefit to significant groups of older people – as the Wider Benefits of Learning research shows. Most people with visual impairment acquire disability with age, and it often marks an end to effective community participation. The same challenges face older people who are deaf or acquire hearing loss. It will be important for the DfES to ensure that older people with other disabilities are not excluded from provision.

The LSC's voluntary and community sector and widening participation strategies should each have a positive impact on older people's provision – but steering that benefit through guidance would be helpful.

As yet the removal of an upper age limit on apprenticeships has not had a significant impact on older adults' opportunities – but DfES may want to consider a later life apprenticeship model for older people planning career changes.

In the same way future tranches of the Union Learning Fund could be targeted at initiatives affecting older workers

Information, Advice and Guidance services should have targets for the engagement of older people, and since older people use Citizens' Advice and Age Concern in large numbers, effective liaison should be secured between information and educational guidance services.

Success for All

There is a clear need for curriculum and pedagogical review and development to ensure that the range of teaching and learning strategies offered are fit for purpose for older learners. NIACE's work on a 'curriculum for later life' can contribute to this. The distinctive needs of 'silver surfers' in particular will need to be considered in the development of teaching and learning strategies for the post-compulsory sector. Good practice will need to be disseminated, and work with older learners included as a core component in tutor training packages.

Every Child Matters

Older adults have a useful role to play in family and inter-generational learning, and in support for children without extended families – both as participants, volunteers and tutors – not least because many have time rich lives

Higher education

The growth in the older learning cohort is already showing the emergence of a small market for recreational engagement with sustained study at higher education. At degree level this is full-cost recoverable. For adults seeking late career change, new courses may need to be developed – perhaps building on the FD formula. Moves to create fair opportunities for part-time students will improve access for many older people; as will the ending of a 54 year old ceiling for access to loans. However, one of the most effective contributions h.e. makes to older people's learning is through continuing education programmes of liberal education. Securing the place of these programmes should be a policy priority.

New Deal for Pensioners/ New Deal for later life

Currently the gap between work and retirement is too stark for many older people to exercise the choices outlined earlier. For many people, the end of a stable period of full-time employment is accompanied by a loss of certainty about identity, and a lack of clarity about future purpose in life. It would be helpful to pilot a programme of learning and learner support able to help older people acquire the skills and identify the pattern of economic and social participation appropriate to their circumstances.

Labour's 1992 manifesto proposal

In 1992 the Labour Party made a manifesto proposal for a 55-plus entitlement to a full year's education for all who had had no post-compulsory education experience was bold. Although few might initially take up such an entitlement it would signal the importance Government gave to learning for a healthy and prolonged older age. It is an idea worth costing.

Stimulating Demand

There is a case for a major campaign to stimulate demand for learning among older people, and to confront wider social attitudes about the value of learning in later life. This could be highlighted within the LSC remit letter. In addition, broadcasters, UfI and the Open University should collaborate on developing a curriculum offer for housebound elders, to ensure that widening participation is not limited to the physically mobile. To monitor reach, new energy should be given to the requirement for LSC to map participation among older people in order to overcome under-representation.

Finally, government should publish an annual participation measure, highlighting the volume of learning in the workplace and in public provision by decades: 45–54, 55–64, 65–74 and 75-plus. Its aim should be to secure rising participation in work and out of it for each cohort until older learners are no longer under-represented.